LIFE ON THE BORDER: EXAMINING BORDER SECURITY THROUGH THE EYES OF LOCAL RESIDENTS AND LAW ENFORCEMENT

FIELD HEARING

BEFORE THE

SUBCOMMITTEE ON BORDER AND MARITIME SECURITY

OF THE

COMMITTEE ON HOMELAND SECURITY HOUSE OF REPRESENTATIVES

ONE HUNDRED FOURTEENTH CONGRESS

SECOND SESSION

MAY 9, 2016

Serial No. 114–67

Printed for the use of the Committee on Homeland Security

Available via the World Wide Web: http://www.gpo.gov/fdsys/

U.S. GOVERNMENT PUBLISHING OFFICE

22–760 PDF   WASHINGTON : 2016

For sale by the Superintendent of Documents, U.S. Government Publishing Office
Internet: bookstore.gpo.gov   Phone: toll free (866) 512–1800; DC area (202) 512–1800
Fax: (202) 512–2104   Mail: Stop IDCC, Washington, DC 20402–0001

COMMITTEE ON HOMELAND SECURITY

MICHAEL T. MCCAUL, Texas, *Chairman*

LAMAR SMITH, Texas
PETER T. KING, New York
MIKE ROGERS, Alabama
CANDICE S. MILLER, Michigan, *Vice Chair*
JEFF DUNCAN, South Carolina
TOM MARINO, Pennsylvania
LOU BARLETTA, Pennsylvania
SCOTT PERRY, Pennsylvania
CURT CLAWSON, Florida
JOHN KATKO, New York
WILL HURD, Texas
EARL L. "BUDDY" CARTER, Georgia
MARK WALKER, North Carolina
BARRY LOUDERMILK, Georgia
MARTHA MCSALLY, Arizona
JOHN RATCLIFFE, Texas
DANIEL M. DONOVAN, JR., New York

BENNIE G. THOMPSON, Mississippi
LORETTA SANCHEZ, California
SHEILA JACKSON LEE, Texas
JAMES R. LANGEVIN, Rhode Island
BRIAN HIGGINS, New York
CEDRIC L. RICHMOND, Louisiana
WILLIAM R. KEATING, Massachusetts
DONALD M. PAYNE, JR., New Jersey
FILEMON VELA, Texas
BONNIE WATSON COLEMAN, New Jersey
KATHLEEN M. RICE, New York
NORMA J. TORRES, California

BRENDAN P. SHIELDS, *Staff Director*
JOAN V. O'HARA, *General Counsel*
MICHAEL S. TWINCHEK, *Chief Clerk*
I. LANIER AVANT, *Minority Staff Director*

———

SUBCOMMITTEE ON BORDER AND MARITIME SECURITY

MARTHA MCSALLY, Arizona, *Chairwoman*

LAMAR SMITH, Texas
MIKE ROGERS, Alabama
CANDICE S. MILLER, MICHIGAN
JEFF DUNCAN, South Carolina
LOU BARLETTA, Pennsylvania
WILL HURD, Texas
MICHAEL T. MCCAUL, Texas *(ex officio)*

FILEMON VELA, Texas
LORETTA SANCHEZ, California
SHEILA JACKSON LEE, Texas
BRIAN HIGGINS, New York
NORMA J. TORRES, California
BENNIE G. THOMPSON, Mississippi *(ex officio)*

PAUL L. ANSTINE, *Subcommittee Staff Director*
JOHN L. DICKHAUS, *Subcommittee Clerk*
ALISON NORTHROP, *Minority Subcommittee Staff Director*

(II)

CONTENTS

LIFE ON THE BORDER: EXAMINING BORDER SECURITY THROUGH THE EYES OF LOCAL RESIDENTS AND LAW ENFORCEMENT

Monday, May 9, 2016

U.S. HOUSE OF REPRESENTATIVES,
COMMITTEE ON HOMELAND SECURITY,
SUBCOMMITTEE ON BORDER AND MARITIME SECURITY,
Sahuarita, AZ.

The subcommittee met, pursuant to call, at 10:01 a.m., in the Council Chambers, Sahuarita Town Hall Building, 375 W. Sahuarita Center Way, Sahuarita, Arizona, Hon. Martha McSally [Chairwoman of the subcommittee] presiding.

Present: Representative McSally.

Also present: Representative Pearce.

Ms. MCSALLY. The Committee on Homeland Security, Subcommittee on Border and Maritime Security, will come to order.

The subcommittee is meeting today to examine border security through the perspective of our local law enforcement, Border Patrol Agents, and residents.

Before we proceed any further, as the Chair, I need to make just a few important announcements.

It takes a tremendous amount of work to put a hearing like this together. I appreciate the interest shown by the number of people who are in attendance today. I also would like to thank the town of Sahuarita for letting us use this beautiful facility for our hearing.

I am now going to recognize myself for an opening statement.

A few weeks ago, I convened my first hearing as the Chairwoman of the Border and Maritime Security Subcommittee on the important topic of border security effectiveness and situational awareness. My subcommittee heard, in Washington, DC, from Border Patrol and CBP air and maritime leadership on the conditions along the border from their vantage point.

The testimony given by these Government officials established further that there seems to be a deep disconnect between what some politicians and policymakers in Washington, DC say about our current situation to secure the border and what I hear on a daily basis back here at home. This is not surprising considering many policymakers in the Nation's capital have never seen or experienced the situation along our border, although we have invited many of them to come visit and see it first-hand. But this is something Southern Arizona residents live with every single day.

At my first hearing, Border Patrol officials stated they have the ability to interdict and apprehend more than 80 percent of the illegal traffic on the Southwest Border, which sounds like an improvement from the last time they measured operational control of the border in 2010, where it stood at 44 percent.

But the Border Patrol numbers only take into account what they see and fail to include all activity, the denominator. So they just have the numerator of what they were able to interdict, not the denominator of everything that is out there. So it is really an incomplete, if not misleading, figure. It does not give an accurate assessment of the current strategy's effectiveness.

At the same hearing, after I pressed them, CBP admitted to having only roughly 50 percent situational awareness of the border and border activity. That means of the illicit activity coming across our Nation's roughly 2,000-mile Southwest Border, CBP only knows what is happening with certainty in about half of it, and that doesn't mean they can interdict what they see. It just means that is what they said they have situational awareness of.

The truth is that the border is not as secure as it needs to be. We all know that here in this room and in this community. And the Department of Homeland Security for years has been trying to sell the American people a false narrative that the border is now more secure than ever.

Local law enforcement, business and community leaders, ranchers and residents, those that I represent who have met with me and spoken to me on countless occasions, you all have a different perspective. You also have a better understanding of the very real border security challenges faced by fellow citizens because you live and work here and experience the ramifications of an unsecure border every day.

Viewing the border through the eyes of local residents, like those before us today, arms policymakers with first-hand experiences on what is and isn't working in border security efforts. At the end of the day, I want to get down to the business of finding thoughtful, common-sense solutions to improve border security.

We are fortunate to have the brave men and women of the Border Patrol do all they can with the tools that they are provided. However, they are often hampered by outdated, flawed strategies or political leadership that doesn't have the resolve to let them do what agents do best, secure the border and protect our communities and the homeland.

Rural border security is a challenging task. Agents do a difficult job, often alone, in rugged terrain. They are subject to a rising number of assaults, which are not frequently prosecuted, and on a daily basis put their lives on the line to prevent cartels from trafficking drugs, money, people, and weapons through our communities.

Local law enforcement officers are often willing and able border security partners, so we need to properly fund and equip them through programs like Operation Stonegarden in order to assist the Federal Government's efforts. Information sharing, joint operations, and collaboration should be the pillars of this approach and will help maximize the results for the whole community.

Every day our fellow citizens, including many in attendance here today, must endure the hassle of border security checkpoints and fear the consequences of illegal activity on their properties, or have their businesses harmed by a perception of the border that does not totally square with reality.

Legislation I authored that recently passed in the House directs the Border Patrol to develop a new strategy that is based on a full assessment of the threats along our Southern Border, including where we have vulnerabilities, the impact of terrain, where we have gaps in situational awareness and operational control, and where the drug cartels are beating us.

Having a frank and honest discussion about what the witnesses see and experience on the border, and their proposed solutions, will help us ensure our Nation's border security efforts protect the citizens who live and work on the border every day, as well as secure the Nation.

We have a very diverse group of witnesses today to provide important perspectives on the challenges, complexities, and solutions regarding border security. As the saying goes, "Where you stand depends upon where you sit," and I think in this case it maybe is adapted to "Where you stand depends upon where you live and where you work," and that I think applies for our witnesses here today.

From reading some of the written statements, or all the written statements, of course, we do have some different viewpoints that will be expressed today from our witnesses, and some disagreements on how to address these issues on a variety of different topics. I look forward to a fruitful, spirited, but respectful discussion and debate on this issue. I would ask that we all consider that we can learn something from each other and maybe find some common ground since we all have, I think, the desire to keep our country and our communities safe. So let's start with that main objective and then figure out how we can find common ground to address these important issues.

I look forward to the testimony of our witnesses today, each of whom brings a unique and important perspective. I want to especially thank my colleague from New Mexico, Mr. Pearce, a fellow Air Force combat pilot as well, by the way. Mr. Pearce represents the 2nd Congressional District of New Mexico, which borders Arizona's 2nd Congressional District to the east and is also home to many miles of the Southwest Border.

[The statement of Chairwoman McSally follows:]

PREPARED STATEMENT OF CHAIRWOMAN MARTHA MCSALLY

MAY 9, 2016

A few weeks ago, I convened my first hearing as the Chairwoman of the Border and Maritime Security Subcommittee on the important topics of border security effectiveness and situational awareness.

My subcommittee heard from Border Patrol and CBP Air and Marine leadership on the conditions along the border from their vantage point.

The testimony given by these Government officials established further that there is a deep disconnect between what politicians and policymakers in Washington, DC say about our current situation to secure the border and what I hear on a daily basis here at home. This is not surprising considering many policy makers in the Nation's capital have never seen or experienced our situation along the border, something Southern Arizona residents live with every day.

At my first hearing, Border Patrol officials stated that they have the ability to interdict and apprehend more than 80% of the illegal traffic on the Southwest Border, which sounds like an improvement from the last time we measured operational control of the border in 2010, which stood at 44%.

But the Border Patrol's numbers only take into account what they see, the numerator, and fail to include all activity, the denominator, so it is an incomplete, if not misleading figure, that does not give an accurate assessment of current strategy's effectiveness.

At the same hearing, after I pressed them, CBP admitted to having only roughly 50% situational awareness of the border. That means, of illicit activity coming across our Nation's roughly 2,000-mile Southwest Border, CBP only knows what is happening with certainty in half of it.

The truth is that the border is not as secure as it needs to be, and the Department of Homeland Security for years has, been trying to sell the American people a false narrative that the border is more secure than ever.

Local law enforcement, business and community leaders, ranchers and residents—those I represent and have met with and spoken to on countless occasions—have a different perspective. They also have a better understanding of the very real border security challenges faced by our fellow citizens because they live and work here and experience the ramifications of an unsecure border every day.

Viewing the border through the eyes of local residents, like those before us today, arms policymakers with first-hand experiences on what is and isn't working in border security efforts. At the end of the day, I want to get down to the business of finding thoughtful, common-sense solutions to improve border security.

We are fortunate to have brave men and women of the Border Patrol do all they can with the tools they are provided. However, they are often hampered by outdated, flawed strategies and political leadership that does not have the resolve to let them do what agents do best—secure the border and protect the homeland.

Rural border security is a difficult task. Agents do a difficult job, often alone, in rugged terrain. They are subject to a rising number of assaults, which are not frequently prosecuted, and on a daily basis put their lives on the line to prevent cartels from trafficking drugs, money, people, and weapons through our communities.

Local law enforcement officers are often willing and able border security partners, so we need to properly fund and equip them through programs like Operation Stonegarden in order to assist the Federal Government's efforts. Information sharing, joint operations and collaboration should be the pillars of this approach and will help maximize the results for the community.

Every day our fellow citizens, including many in attendance here today, must endure the hassle of a border security checkpoints, fear the consequences of illegal activity on their property, or have their businesses harmed by a perception of the border that does not totally square with reality.

Legislation I authored that recently passed in the House directs the Border Patrol to develop a new strategy that is based on a full assessment of the threats along our Southern Border, including where we have vulnerabilities, the impact of terrain, where we have gaps in situational awareness and operational control, and where the drug cartels are beating us.

Having a frank and honest discussion about what the witnesses see and experience on the border, and their proposed solutions will help us ensure our Nation's border security efforts protect the citizens who live and work on the border every day, as well as secure the Nation.

We have a very diverse group of witnesses today to provide important perspectives on the challenges, complexities, and solutions regarding border security. As the saying goes: "Where you stand depends upon where you sit" and maybe for this topic, perhaps it should be "where you stand depends upon where you live and work."

From reading the written statements, we have some different viewpoints and disagreements between some of our witnesses on a variety of topics. I look forward to a fruitful, spirited, but respectful discussion and debate. I would ask that we all consider that we can learn from each other today and find common ground, since we all have the desire to keep our country and communities safe.

I very much look forward to the testimony of our witnesses today, each of whom brings a unique and important perspective to this discussion. I want to especially welcome the gentleman from New Mexico, Mr. Pearce, to Arizona. Mr. Pearce represents the 2nd Congressional District of New Mexico, which borders Arizona's 2nd Congressional District to the east and is also home to many miles of the Southwest Border.

Ms. MCSALLY. I now want to recognize the gentleman from New Mexico, Mr. Pearce, for any opening statement you may have.

Mr. PEARCE. Thank you. I will just be brief. Thanks for not saying also that you flew in this millennium and I flew in the last millennium.

[Laughter.]

Mr. PEARCE. So I appreciate you leaving that part out.

When you deal with the voters, which we have to do every 2 years, you start to understand that they don't really want to focus too much on the exact circumstances of bills and legislation. Instead, it is like the tide moving back and forth. I will guarantee you that people in this country right now do not feel safe.

So Washington can say the border is secure all they want, and I appreciate reading your testimony, sir, that says that we have work to do and we need to be more transparent, more honest. I think that the beginning point is exactly what we are doing here, getting all the stakeholders together. Congresswoman McSally came in and immediately took a lead role in this.

Her district and mine butt up against each other. I am just across the end of New Mexico all the way to El Paso, and we see very strong similarities, and you just have the sense here that the closer you get to the border, the more that people are just very unsettled. We as a Nation need to be dealing with that unsettlement.

Of course, the problem is that some people want to solve it one way and some another. So the testimony that I have read today— and I really appreciate the balance that you have on the panels, because that is one of the keys—you can't just approach it from one direction. So I am looking forward to it.

I would just tell you frankly that I think both parties have gamed this issue for years. So the fact that it is here and we are dealing with it in the fashion that the anger has reached the level that it has just tells us it is time to get to work and do what we were sent there to do, make hard decisions about very difficult things in a pragmatic and sensible way.

So I am looking forward to the discussion and seeing what we come up with.

Thanks again. I appreciate the invitation to be here.

Ms. MCSALLY. Absolutely. Thanks.

Okay, so we have 2 panels today. The first panel has 3 people on it, and the second panel has 5 people on it. We tried to group them, generally speaking. We have elected officials, our Cochise County Sheriff, and Mr. Del Cueto is representing the Border Patrol Agents. So this is kind of the official perspective, if that makes sense, the public-sector perspective. Then the second panel has a mix of individuals that are from the community and the private sector providing different perspectives. So I just wanted to lay that groundwork.

I do want to acknowledge we do have the Pima County Sheriff Nanos here in the audience. We appreciate you coming for our discussion here today.

So first I will give a couple of introductions and bios here.

Sheriff Mark Dannels is the sheriff of Cochise County, Arizona, a position he has held since November 2012. Sheriff Dannels began his law enforcement career in 1984 after serving in the United

States Army and progressed through the ranks within Cochise County Sheriff's Office after working numerous specialty assignments and leadership roles. He is a member of numerous organizations, including the Fraternal Order of Police, the National Sheriffs Association, the Southwest Border Sheriffs Association, and the Arizona Homeland Security Regional Advisory Council.

Mayor Danny Ortega is the mayor of Douglas, Arizona. Mayor Ortega was born and raised in Douglas, and also serves as the vice president of his family-owned business that was first established in Douglas in 1923. He has been involved in many organizations in the Douglas community, including the Douglas Chamber of Commerce and the Douglas Lion's Club.

Mr. Art Del Cueto is the president of the Border Patrol Union Local 2544. Mr. Del Cueto has been a Border Patrol Agent since 2003 and began his career in Casa Grande, Arizona, where he helped in the effort to establish a new substation at Three Points, Arizona. Prior to working for the Border Patrol, Mr. Del Cueto worked in a maximum security state prison in Tucson.

The witnesses' full written testimony will appear in the record.

The Chair now recognizes Sheriff Dannels for his verbal testimony.

STATEMENT OF MARK DANNELS, SHERIFF, COCHISE COUNTY, ARIZONA

Sheriff DANNELS. Good morning, everyone. Chairwoman McSally, Mr. Pearce, thank you for having us today, and thank you, both of you, for just your awareness and support in these issues.

With me today is also Pima County Sheriff Chris Nanos, who is sitting to my right. He is the Pima County Sheriff here who works closely with us on the Southwest Border Task Force.

With 83 miles of international border within its jurisdiction, Cochise County plays a significant role in combating drug and human trafficking organizations and the associated violent crime which adversely affects Arizona residents and other areas throughout the United States. With 6,219 square miles, Cochise County is the 38th-largest land mass county in the United States.

One of Mexico's largest and most notorious trafficking organizations and drug cartels, the Sinaloa Cartel, has long employed the use of local Mexican drug trafficking organizations, DTOs, to carry out the cartel's drug distribution and transportation in and throughout the United States. The Mexican drug trafficking organizations operating in Cochise County are highly sophisticated and innovative in their transportation methods. Violence against innocent citizens, public officials, law enforcement, and rival drug/human trafficking groups in Mexico continues to escalate.

The adverse effects of the drug and human trafficking organizations operating in Cochise County not only have significantly diminished the quality of life of county residents but also placed unbearable financial strain upon the budgets and resources of private and Government agencies in the county.

Having the true-life experience to live and work as a law enforcement officer/deputy and now sheriff in Cochise County since 1984, it has been an educational lesson for me to reference border security in the evolution of this border. I have witnessed the escalation of violence by these careless assailants on our citizens, raising the question: Who actually controls our borders? Cochise County has become known as the gateway to illegal activity for those unlawfully entering into the United States.

In the history of the border, which I think is critical to where we are at today, in the early 1990s the Federal Government came up with a plan to address the unsecure, unsafe border. I call it the plan of the Ps, and that was to protect the populated areas—Yuma, El Paso, and San Diego were targeted cities—along with the ports of entry.

The other half of the plan, which is the disturbing part of the plan, was to re-route that illegal activity into the rural parts of the Southwest Border. Mr. Pearce, your area, as you know, in New Mexico is a highly-trafficked area, just like Cochise County, Santa Cruz County, and other parts of the Southwest Border.

Since that time there have been many changes, since the early '90s, with this plan being in place. We have had some successes, and that is a reduction in those protected "P" areas. Unfortunately, we have had increased illegal activity in the outside protected areas, outside the ports and populated areas, to include Cochise County. We have had fear and frustration increase in rural Cochise County along the Southwest Border, ranch and farmlands damaged due to increased illegal activity, property damage—fencing, livestock, water lines. Burglaries and thefts in rural Cochise County are on the rise. Violent crimes include homicides, assaults, rapes, drug smuggling, et cetera. Transnational cartels and smuggling organizations have actually controlled and set up smuggling routes throughout Cochise County, which is on-going as we speak.

Lack of redefinition of the plan since the 1990s, there has been no redefinition to this plan for over 20 years.

Economic decline. Cochise County is losing population at a staggering rate. We were No. 1 population decrease several years ago. I believe we are going to be No. 1 in the country again for population decrease.

Legacy ranchers, I think we have had a half-dozen to a dozen ranches sold in the last few years.

Lack of Federally-elected leaders to address insecure borders. Fear is creating a lack of trust and anger by citizens in Cochise County along the border.

Questionable consequences by Federal Government by those committing border crimes.

Undue pressure on local law enforcement sheriffs to address these issues; fear and consequences for committing border crimes.

Lack of funding for local law enforcement, the criminal justice system, corrections, our jails, in order to address border crimes at the local level due to the Federal Government's lack of intervention.

Local solutions and programs are no longer a thought but a mandate. Many sheriffs on the Southwest Border, to include Cochise County, have taken our statutory and elected oath seriously in the fact to protect their freedoms and liberties. We have enacted many programs, balanced community policing through education and prevention and enforcement; transparency plus time, we built community trust; collaborated efforts coming from the local side with all

3 levels of government; installation of new radio towers, radios; working with our schools, 21 rural schools, where they are all getting radios here in the next few months; ranchers and citizens that live in the vulnerable areas, we are going to be issuing them radios.

A regional application for law enforcement where we are sharing together. We have a financial interdiction unit working on financial crimes, along with a regional border team supported by the Border Patrol.

A ranch advisory team where 2 deputies are taken off patrol to work with the ranchers so they have an ear and a voice on that, a ranch advisory team made up of ranchers throughout Cochise County to help us enhance communication; and consequence-driven prosecution. I will give you an example of what I am talking about with that.

The Federal Government has an issue prosecuting juveniles based on their laws. We started this several months ago where we have an average of 26 juveniles, ages 14 to 17, in my jail that are now being prosecuted as adults and being sent to prison for a year-and-a-half, and these are ones when the Border Patrol picks up a backpacker, they turn them over to the Sheriff's Department or a local agency who makes the arrest, and then we prosecute them through our local county attorneys, a partnership that is called a righteous partnership. Before this was going on, these vulnerable youth, both on the local side from our local high school and from across the line, were being recruited by the cartels to smuggle drugs into the United States. We took a prevention and enforcement approach toward that.

The Federal Government and elected policymakers have been slow to react to the voices and concerns of those living on the Southwest Border. The following comprehensive recommendations are directly linked to our Federal leaders and given to you based on what we see.

Re-define the plan of the '90s and build upon its successes.

There needs to be a political will to make border security a mandated program and not a discretionary one.

Border security first, immigration reform second.

Secondary checkpoints only after primary border interdiction is satisfied by the stakeholders.

Quality of life/citizens living on the border supported by sheriffs and State governors regarding improved security and safety.

Funding supplement for local law enforcement, prosecution, detention, criminal justice in support of border crimes.

SCAP needs to be enhanced. Right now it is at 4.8 cents on the dollar for reimbursing sheriffs to hold illegals.

Continued funding and support for Stonegarden program—it has been a success, and please don't remove that—to include the EREs and employee-related expenses that go with that. That is very important to rural counties.

Enhanced funding for regional communication and interoperability with local law enforcement.

There is a staggering number of—an article came out here where in 2015, 19,000 criminal aliens were released back into communities in the United States. That is a lose/lose for every sheriff and police chief in this country, and for the morale of the men and women who serve in our Border Patrol, which we have a great relationship in our county.

The recipe for success for this problem starts at the local level first. Our local efforts have proven to be beneficial in bringing overdue solutions to an unsecure border that has become a discretionary program by those Federally-elected leaders and policymakers that have been entrusted to protect our freedoms and liberties. As a sheriff elected by the good people of my county, my biggest fear is another loss of life to one of my citizens and/or law enforcement officers/agents contributed to a border that is not secure. One would hope the priority of securing our border doesn't become just about a price tag and/or political posturing, but rather the legal and moral requirement to safeguard all of America, which so many heroic Americans have already paid the ultimate price for.

Today's opportunity to address this group instills fresh hope that our voice does matter, and on behalf of the citizens of Cochise County, the Southwest Border sheriffs, Arizona sheriffs and beyond, we hope you won't forget us and will do your Constitutional mandate to bring positive change to an overdue vulnerable situation.

With that, I leave you an open invitation, Mr. Pearce. I know Ms. McSally has been down there numerous times. Her and I have spoken and driven around, and she actually has not seen a show-and-tell border but a real border.

Thank you.

[The prepared statement of Sheriff Dannels follows:]

PREPARED STATEMENT OF MARK DANNELS

MAY 9, 2016

INTRODUCTION

Chairwoman Martha McSally and Members of this committee, thank you for the invitation to speak to you today on this very important subject.

HISTORY OF COCHISE COUNTY

With 83 miles of international border within its jurisdiction, Cochise County plays a significant role in combating drug and human trafficking organizations and the associated violent crime which adversely affects Arizona residents and other areas throughout the United States. In 1990 the Office of National Drug Control Policy (ONDCP) designated Cochise County as a High-Intensity Drug Trafficking Area within southern Arizona. This designation is a direct result of overwhelming and sustained levels of illicit drug and human trafficking within Cochise County.

With 6,219 square miles, Cochise County is as large as the States of Rhode Island and Connecticut combined. The estimated population of the county in 2010 is approximately 131,346. The geography of the county consists of 7 incorporated cities to include the historical town of Tombstone. Surrounded by vast areas of desolate uninhabited desert and mountainous terrain, the 7 cities only represent a combined area of 215 square miles, leaving 6,004 square miles of unincorporated area. These desolate areas are routinely exploited for smuggling routes by the drug/human traffickers and pose one of the greatest challenges to local law enforcements effort in establishing border security and interdiction efforts. Cochise County is the 38th-largest land mass county in the United States, and is home to the United States Army base, Fort Huachuca. Throughout the history of the county ranching and farming has played a significant part in its legacy.

Unlike other border counties in Arizona, Cochise County is unique in that there are 2 cities in the Republic of Mexico situated on the international border within the county. The cities of Agua Prieta and Naco, with an estimated population of 80,000 and 10,000 respectively, are well know to U.S. Law Enforcement officials as staging and operational centers for one of Mexico's largest and most notorious drug cartels. The Sinaloa Cartel has long employed the use of local Mexican drug trafficking organizations (DTO's) to carry out the cartel's drug distribution and transportation into and throughout the United States.

These local DTO's also utilize their established smuggling routes in Cochise County to transport the cartels illicit profits such as U.S. currency, firearms, and ammunition into Mexico. A large portion of the profit is used to sustain control over the corridor through the use of violence against law enforcement, rival trafficking organizations, and bribes of government officials.

The Mexican drug trafficking organizations operating in Cochise County are highly sophisticated and innovative in their transportation methods. Aside from the normal use of human backpackers (mules), clandestine tunnels, and vehicles, the trafficking organizations have resorted to the use of ultra light aircraft which cannot be detected by normal radar, cloned vehicles appearing to be law enforcement or other legitimate companies, and most recently the use of catapults which hurl bundles of marijuana into the United States to awaiting co-conspirators. The organizations utilize sophisticated and technical communications and counter surveillance equipment to counter law enforcements interdiction tactics and strategies. Scouts or observers are strategically placed along smuggling routes to perform counter surveillance on law enforcement and report their observations to those controlling the drug/human smuggling operation so they may avoid and elude law enforcement. The use of cell phones and sophisticated two-way radio encryptions for communications are standard equipment, as are night vision and forward looking infra-red devices.

Violence against innocent citizens, public officials, law enforcement, and rival drug/human trafficking groups in Mexico continues to escalate. Cochise County's law enforcement and private citizen fears of it spilling into the county were realized in 2010 when a long-time Cochise County resident rancher was senselessly murdered while inspecting fences on his ranch. Further complicating the concerns is the potential for foreign terrorist to employ drug/human trafficking organizations to smuggle individuals and or weapons of mass destruction into the United States through Cochise County.

The adverse affects of the drug and human trafficking organizations operating in Cochise County not only have significantly diminished the quality of life of county residents, but also placed unbearable strain upon the budgets and resources of private and government agencies in the county.

Historically speaking, illegal border crossings into the United States are well-known in southern Arizona and recognized as a part of everyday life within Cochise County and throughout the Southwest Border. Many years ago, Cochise County citizens were not overly alarmed when they observed a handful of undocumented aliens travelling through private or public lands in search of jobs. Unfortunately, over time these groups dramatically increased in size and became more reckless, aggressive, and violent, bringing unrest and fear to the citizens living on the border. Examples of this include reckless high speed pursuits, assaults on citizens, rapes, kidnappings, murders, and home invasions to steal one's private and personal possessions. It was apparent the search for the American dream was being over-shadowed by these mules, coyotes, bandits, and transnational criminals preying upon our citizens.

Having the true-life experience to live and work as a law enforcement officer/deputy and now Sheriff in Cochise County since 1984, it has been an educational lesson for me reference border security. I have witnessed the escalation of violence by these careless assailants on our citizens raising the question, who actually controls our borders? Cochise County has become known as the gateway to illegal activity for those unlawfully entering into the United States.

FEDERAL GOVERNMENT'S BORDER SECURITY PLAN OF THE '90S

In the early 1990s, the Federal Government prepared a plan to address the unsecure, unsafe border. At a press conference in Tucson, Arizona, a Border Patrol spokesman announced their intent to secure the populated areas of the border, specifically San Diego, Yuma and El Paso and the International Ports of Entry. These targeted areas, which I call the "Ps=Ports and Population", would be the Federal Government's focus points. The second half of their plan was to reroute the illegal activity/disturbances into the rural parts of the Southwest Border with the thought that these cartel organizations and smuggling groups would be deterred by the rugged and mountainous regions along the border.

Since the release of the plan, many changes have taken place. Specifically, Cochise County has increased their staffing of Border Patrol agents from a handful of agents to an estimated 1,300 agents stationed within Cochise County. To add, an estimated 200 Customs agents working at the port of entries (Douglas and Naco) and within the Cochise County to secure and protect the estimated 83 miles of international border. Infrastructure, such as metal fencing, lightning, cameras, sensors, radars, etc. have been installed between both ports and some distance beyond bringing some needed relief to this area and those that live within. Secondary immigration checkpoints were established on routes (roadways) 20–40 miles north of the border. The plan has been in place for over 20 years and the following are some thoughts regarding the plan:

- Reduction in illegal activity between the protected areas (ports)
- Decrease in larger groups of undocumented aliens between the protected areas (ports)
- Increase in illegal activity outside the protected areas (ports)
- Fear/Frustration increased in rural Cochise County/Southwest Border
- Ranch and Farm lands damaged due to increased illegal activity
- Property (fencing, livestock, waterlines, etc.) damaged
- Burglaries/Thefts increased in rural Cochise County/Southwest Border
- Violent Crimes increased i.e. Homicides, Assaults, Rapes, Drug and Human Smuggling, etc. in rural Cochise County/Southwest Border
- Transnational Cartels/Smuggling Organizations controlled and set up smuggling routes in rural Cochise County/Southwest Border
- Lack of Border Patrol Agents directly on border but north of border
- Secondary checkpoints became international ports within communities resulting in disturbances/illegal activity during all hours of the day or night
- Lack of Re-Definition to the plan of the '90s (time erased history)
- Loss of recreational land use due to fear of criminal activity
- Economic decline (Cochise County largest decrease in population)
- Legacy Ranches being sold
- Lack of Federally-elected leaders to address unsecure border/fears creating a lack of trust and anger by citizens
- Questionable consequences by Federal Government by those committing border crimes
- Undue pressure on local law enforcement/Sheriffs to address issues, fear, and consequences for those committing crimes
- Lack of funding for local law enforcement/criminal justice system/corrections in order to address border crimes at the local level due to Federal Government lack of intervention
- Border Security shall be a Mandate, not a Discretionary program
- Border Security v. Immigration Reform (two different programs not to be blended)
- Lack of Trust and Confidence in Federal Government=Border Patrol as arm of Federal Government

ACTION-BASED SOLUTIONS LOCAL GOVERNMENT

Local Solutions and Programs are no longer a thought, but a reality for bringing relief to our citizens who consciously choose to live near our borders. No better example of the importance of local law enforcement during a National crisis was the terrorist attack on September 11, 2001. First responders from local police and fire were the first on scene to address this horrific threat. Local law enforcement is best-suited to best understand community needs and solutions based on the expectations of their citizens. Community policing begins and succeeds at the local level first.

As the Sheriff of Cochise County, I felt it was my elected and statutory duty (oath of office to support the United States Constitution and the Arizona Constitution) to protect and secure the freedoms and liberties of my citizens, with or without the help of our Federal law enforcement partners/policy makers. No longer a debate by those that live in the rural parts of the Southwest Border, the rural parts of the Southwest Border are NOT secure and are vulnerable for ANY type of transnational criminal activity.

Working with limited budgets and staffing, sheriffs along the Southwest Border struggle each and every day to find ways to enhance the quality of life/safety for those they serve and bring a general sense of deterrence for those choosing our border as a venue to promote their criminal enterprises. The following bullet points are action-driven solutions implemented in hopes of bringing some relief and sense of security for those living in Cochise County:

- Balanced Community Policing (Education, Prevention, Enforcement)
- Transparency+Time=Community Trust
- Collaborated Efforts by all 3-levels of Government
- Law and Order Partnership between Sheriff and County Attorney

- Private and Public Funding donations/grants to purchase upgraded equipment/communications
- Installation of New Radios/Towers/Consoles/Microwave
- Portable Radios to Citizens/Ranchers/Farmers/Schools
- Interoperability/Intelligence Sharing at all 3 levels
- Regional Application for Law Enforcement
- Financial Interdiction Unit
- Regional Border Team by Sheriff supported by Border Patrol, ICE, U.S. Forest
- Ranch Advisory Team
- Ranch Patrol
- Consequence-Driven Prosecution (all 3 levels)
- Local Trail-Cameras, Sensors, ATVs, Thermal Vehicle, Off-Road Vehicle, etc.
- Factual Situational Awareness for Media, Elected Officials, America
- Quarterly Law Enforcement Leadership Meetings
- Community Outreach Unit
- Community Meet & Greets within Communities
- Aviation Program (Helicopter & Drone)
- Positive-Interactive Use of Media and Social Media

RECOMMENDATIONS FEDERAL GOVERNMENT

The Federal Government (elected and policy makers) has been slow to react to the voices and concerns of those living on the Southwest Border. Cochise County and other counties along the border have become VIP attractions, venues for those seeking to make a difference or promising change only to become another faded high-hope. The following comprehensive recommendations are directly linked to our Federal leaders:

- Re-define the plan of the '90s and build upon successes
- Political Will to make Border Security a Mandated Program
- Border Security First, Immigration Reform Second
- Maximize Allocated Resources such as Staffing (only 43% of Border Agents in the Tucson Sector are assigned on the border)
- Support and Embrace First-line Agents that work the border regions, they have a dangerous job and it's no secret that their frustration is high based on the unknown complexities reference their assignments, they have great ideas to share
- Secondary Checkpoints only after Primary border interdiction is satisfied by stakeholders
- Quality in Life/Citizens living on border supported by Sheriffs and State Governors regarding improved security/safety
- Funding supplement for Local Law Enforcement/Prosecution/Detention/Criminal Justice in support of border crimes
- Continued Funding and Support for Stone Garden Program
- Empowerment with action to Border Patrol Leadership/PACs (currently Cochise County has 3-dedicated and solution-driven leaders that work well with local law enforcement)
- Enhanced Funding for Regional Communication and Interoperability with local law enforcement
- Cultural/Quality in Service Training for Border Patrol Agents working in rural counties

SUMMARY

Our local efforts have proven to be beneficial in bringing over-due solutions to an unsecure border that has become a discretionary program by those Federally-elected leaders and policy makers that have been entrusted to protect our freedoms and liberties. As a Sheriff elected by the good people of my county, my biggest fear is another loss of life to one of my citizens and/or law enforcement officers/agents contributed to a border that is NOT secure. One would hope the priority of securing our border doesn't become just about a price tag and/or political posturing, but rather the legal and moral requirement to safeguard all of America, which so many heroic Americans have already paid the ultimate price for.

Today's opportunity to address this group instills fresh hope that our voice does matter and on behalf of the citizens of Cochise County, Arizona and beyond, we hope you won't forget us and will do your Constitutional mandate to bring positive change to an over-due vulnerable situation.

I will leave each one of you with an open invitation to visit Cochise County along with a personal-guided tour and visit with our citizens to hear/see first-hand America's true rural border.

Again, thank you very much for the opportunity to share this information with you. I will be happy to answer any questions you may have.

ATTACHMENT.—LETTER FROM THE ARIZONA SHERIFFS ASSOCIATION

July 28, 2014, Phoenix, Arizona.

This letter is authored by the Arizona Sheriffs Association to address the lack of border security on the part of our Federal Government, thereby placing our Arizona citizens and all those that visit our beautiful State in harm's way by those that have chosen to infringe upon and violate our freedoms and liberties as guaranteed under the U.S. Constitution.

Arizona Sheriffs are standing united and steadfast in support of "Secure and Safe" borders in hopes of enhancing public safety for our Arizona citizens and all Americans. A "Secure and Safe" border is one that provides a genuine deterrent for those that cross into our country illegally and for illicit gain.

Border security must never be a discretionary program, but a mandate by our Federal leaders and policy makers. The quality of life normally enjoyed by our citizens has been jeopardized by an unsecure border that enables transnational criminals and their accomplices to prey on our citizens.

Our focus is border security and is NOT to be confused with immigration reform.

SHERIFF MARK DANNELS,
Cochise County.
SHERIFF LEON WILMOT,
Yuma County.
SHERIFF CLARENCE DUPNIK,
Pima County.
SHERIFF TONY ESTRADA,
Santa Cruz County.
SHERIFF JOHN DRUM,
La Paz County.
SHERIFF PRESTON "PJ" ALLRED,
Graham County.
SHERIFF LARRY AVILA,
Greenlee County.
SHERIFF ADAM SHEPHERD,
Gila County.
SHERIFF JOE ARPAIO,
Maricopa County.
SHERIFF PAUL BABEU,
Pinal County.
SHERIFF SCOTT MASCHER,
Yavapai County.
SHERIFF KELLY "KC" CLARK,
Navajo County.
SHERIFF TOM SHEAHAN,
Mohave County.
SHERIFF JOSEPH DEDMAN,
Apache County.
SHERIFF BILL PRIBIL,
Coconino County.

Ms. MCSALLY. Thank you, Sheriff Dannels.
The Chair now recognizes Mayor Ortega to testify.

STATEMENT OF DANNY ORTEGA, MAYOR, DOUGLAS, ARIZONA

Mr. ORTEGA. Thank you, Chairwoman McSally, Representative Pearce. Thanks for joining us here today.

I am mayor of Douglas, Arizona, and also a businessman. My family came to Douglas in the early 1920s and established a shoe business there, and we have been running it ever since. We have been very active in our community as a family, and myself personally as well.

When you come to our town, I hope you see security through our eyes. I think the residents of our community feel very safe in Douglas, and we have many binational events with the sister city of Agua Prieta. We recently had a binational concert that drew hundreds of people where a band played on the Mexican side and then followed by a band on the American side.

I understand the need for more security away from the ports of entry, but we cannot let that get in the way of the legal crossing of goods and people. As I have often heard, we need high fences and wider gates. We also need to talk about making it more efficient and easier to trade goods and services with Mexico. Total U.S. goods traded with Mexico in 2013 equaled $506.6 billion, and growing at close to 5 percent. Mexico is the third-ranked commercial trading partner with the United States and the second-largest market for U.S. export. Trade with Mexico sustains 6 million jobs in the United States. Sales to Mexico are larger than all U.S. exports to Brazil, Russia, India, and China combined. Twenty-two U.S. States count Mexico as their No. 1 or 2 trading partner in exports, and a top-5 market to 14 other States as well.

For every dollar Mexico makes from exporting to the United States, it will turn 50 cents in U.S. products or services, which helps our struggling economy. In May 2010, the United States and Mexico signed the 21st Century Border Management Joint Declaration recognizing the importance of developing a modern and secure border infrastructure to make us both more competitive in the global market.

Our ports are antiquated and we do not have the staffing to support the growing trade and border crosses at our southern ports of entry. We have struggled and are making do with what limited resources we have, yet are unable to handle the projected growth without more bodies and money at our ports.

Border towns have been ignored for many years even though we provide access to one of the fastest-growing economies in the world. China is starting to have better relations with Mexico and is one of our biggest competitors for the burgeoning economy. We need to view the Southern Border as an asset and not a liability.

Locally in Douglas, our current port was built in 1936, with minor upgrades done in 1993. We have outgrown the facility and put the officers and people crossing at risk. If there is ever a chemical spill at our current port, we do not have a HAZMAT facility that could control such a spill. We ship many chemicals to the mines in Mexico. We have trucks waiting for extended periods of time, polluting the air with exhaust. We do not have modern equipment to inspect trucks or cars because of the lack of funding and space.

Douglas is considered a small port, yet over $1.5 billion worth of merchandise crosses our port on a yearly basis, and that number is growing at about 5 percent over the last 5 years. We have seen growth in industry of about 40 percent in the past 5 years, and that growth is starting to show on the American side. We currently applied for a new port of entry. We think we need to take the commercial port out of our local footprint. Congresswoman McSally has been very supportive of that effort, and we thank you for that.

The cattle industry is also very large in our area. We currently cross about 1,500 head of cattle a day in the peak season of November to May. That is over $2 million a day in cattle crossings to help support the American appetite for beef. We need some investment in our ports of entry. The road for the cattle pen is currently a dirt road that is not maintained, and we are looking to work with some of our local investors to see how we can improve that port.

We also need to streamline the process in which Mexican citizens have the ability to obtain a B1 or B2 border crossing card to come to the United States, shop, and visit our communities on a legal basis. Sixty-five percent of our revenue for the city of Douglas comes from sales tax, and 80 percent of that money comes from the Mexican consumer. We need help in just getting people across the border, back and forth.

I have spoken to many friends on the Mexican side. Many are proud to be Mexican. They do not want to come and live here. They just want to come here and shop, visit our country, and then go back home.

There is a net loss in migration currently, according to the Pew Institute. More people are actually—Mexicans are leaving our country versus coming into our country, and we hope we can just leave this meeting today with the thought that we need easier access for people and goods and services to come across. We really need investment in the infrastructure, our ports of entry and our roads.

Thank you for listening to me today, and I will entertain any questions later. Thank you.

[The prepared statement of Mr. Ortega follows:]

PREPARED STATEMENT OF DANNY ORTEGA

MAY 9, 2016

Good morning and thank you for taking time for visiting our border community. I was born and raised in a border town, Douglas, AZ. my family first arrived in Douglas in the early 1920's and have always been active members of the community. When you come to our town I hope you see security through our eyes, those of us who live and work every day miles from Mexico. I understand the need for more security away from the ports of entry but we cannot let that affect the legal crossing of goods and people. As I have often heard we need high fences and wider gates we also need to talk about making it more efficient and easier to trade goods and services with Mexico. Total U.S. goods trade with Mexico in 2013 equaled $506.6 billion and growing at close to 5%. Mexico is the third-ranked commercial trading partner with the United States and the second-largest market for U.S. exports. Trade with Mexico sustains 6 million jobs in the United States. Sales to are larger than all U.S. exports to Brazil, Russia, India, and China combined. Twenty-two States count Mexico as their No. 1 or 2 export market and a top 5 market to 14 other States. For every dollar Mexico makes from exporting to the United States, it will in turn spend 50 cents on U.S. products or services, which helps our struggling economy. In May of 2010 the United States and Mexico signed the 21st Century Border Management Joint Declaration recognizing the importance of developing a modern secure border infrastructure to make us both more competitive in the global economy. Our ports are antiquated and we do not have the staffing to support the growing trade and border crossers at our southern ports of entry. We have struggled and are making due with the limited resources yet we will not be able to handle the projected growth without more bodies and money in our ports. Border towns have been ignored for many years even though we provide access to one of the fastest-growing economies in the world. China is starting to have better relations with Mexico and is one of our biggest competitors for the burgeoning economy. We need to view the Southern Border as an asset and not a liability.

Locally in Douglas our current port was built in 1936 with minor upgrades done in 1993. We have outgrown the facility and put the officers and people crossing at risk. If there is ever a chemical spill at our port we do not have a HAZMAT facility that could control such a spill. We have trucks waiting for extended periods of time polluting the air with their exhaust. We do not have the modern equipment to inspect trucks because of a lack of funding and space. Douglas is considered a small port of entry and yet over $1.5 billion worth of merchandise crosses our port on a yearly basis and that number is growing at about 5% over the last 5 years. We have seen growth in the maquiladora industry of about 40% in the past year on the Mexican side and are starting to experience similar growth in Douglas. These are good jobs for our community.

The cattle industry is huge in the Mexican state of Sonora, in Douglas alone we cross about 1,500 head of cattle a day in the peak season of November through May. These cattle are headed for States in the Midwest for fattening and eventually to be served in our restaurants. We currently have a dirt road providing access to the cattle pens which is not maintained and many times washes out in the rainy season. This equates to over $2 million a day in cattle crossing, supporting the American appetite for beef. We could use some investment in the infrastructure for this valuable cattle crossing.

We also need help in streamlining the process in which Mexican citizens have the ability to obtain a B1/B2 Border Crossing Card (B1 Visitor for Business and B2 for Visitor) visa to come to the United States to shop and visit our communities. As a community in Arizona we rely heavily on sales tax for city services. About 65% of our general funds come from sales tax revenue and 80% of our sales come from Mexico. We are very fluid communities both depending on each other for survival, meaning efficient cross-border crossings is important. Our ports of entry are not designed for south-bound inspections which have been enforced within the last 6 years. We put not only the inspectors at risk but also the citizens who have to wait in line for several hours to travel what may be a mile. We have no efficient system in place to see who is crossing south-bound. This truly discourages people from travelling into both our communities affecting local commerce on both sides of the border.

There is a net loss in net migration according to the Pew institute. I truly believe that most Mexicans want to live in Mexico but come to the United States to earn a decent living, as the Mexican economy is growing we are seeing more Mexican citizens staying home. We are seeing the drug traffic increase and the number of human smugglers is decreasing. I hope that you leave here today realizing that the border is an asset to our country and that it needs investment in many areas, we have contributed much to the U.S. economy and feel that we deserve some investment. We would like to have more of a voice in decisions being made and we thank you for taking the time to coming here and listening.

Ms. MCSALLY. Thanks, Mayor Ortega.

For the record, I just want to make a comment, that the second hearing we had in Washington, DC last month was really focusing on the infrastructure and the staffing at our ports of entry, which has been a critical issue for us in our community, and really across the country, and identifying what we can do to speed up the hiring of the CBP Officers, as well as upgrading the infrastructure project. We very much have been working closely on that and are dialing on that. Today we are trying to focus on the in-between the ports and the security issues there, but it is important to have the full picture of our witnesses as we are sort-of framing the discussion. So I just want to highlight that we are not ignoring that issue in this particular hearing, but I just wanted to frame that, especially for our audience.

The Chair now recognizes Mr. Del Cueto to testify.

STATEMENT OF ART DEL CUETO, PRESIDENT, LOCAL 2544, NATIONAL BORDER PATROL COUNCIL

Mr. DEL CUETO. Chairwoman McSally, Congressman Pearce, thank you for providing me the opportunity to testify on behalf of the National Border Patrol Council and on behalf of Local 2544, the union here in Tucson, Arizona. The National Border Patrol Council represents the interests of 16,500 line agents at the Border Patrol.

My name is Art Del Cueto. I am a native of Douglas, Arizona and have been with the Border Patrol since 2003.

One of the many areas in which the Border Patrol excels is in keeping statistics. The Border Patrol can tell you in detail how many agents we have. They can tell you the number of overtime hours that are worked, the number of apprehensions, or the hours of air support delivered by CBP air and marine operations. It is really quite impressive. If I was a Member of Congress from a non-border State and I sat through a CBP briefing about how the border was secure, I would be inclined to believe them.

The primary statistic that Commissioner Kerlikowske talks about today in support of his belief that the border is secure is the number of apprehensions, which is down. At the height of illegal immigration in 2000, Border Patrol apprehended 1.6 million people. In the Tucson sector alone that year, we arrested 616,000 illegal immigrants. To put this in perspective, the entire population of Tucson in 2000 was 486,000. That was how massive this influx was.

Back in 2000, we were facing a wave of Mexican economic migrants in search of employment. There was little organization and most illegal immigrants simply loaded up a backpack of supplies, jumped the border and headed north. This lack of organization frankly made them relatively easy to catch if you could deploy Border Patrol manpower.

Fast-forward to 2016 and the entire border is controlled by the Mexican drug cartels. The drug cartels control the border in the same way that most prisons are controlled by the inmates. Nothing moves along this border without their permission, and illegal aliens and narcotics are simply 2 lines of business within that same organization.

Here in Arizona, we have the Sinaloa Cartel. The 63,000 individuals that we arrested last year in this sector paid the cartel a considerable amount of money just to cross in our area. Only based on the individuals we arrested in this sector, the Sinaloa Cartel made millions from illegal alien smuggling. If there is one point that I want to make in this entire testimony it is that the money that the cartels earn from illegal smuggling underwrites the exact same organizations that are flooding our streets with narcotics. Money is flowing back to the same organizations that are responsible for the violence in Mexico which has murdered over 150,000 people. It is going back to the same organizations that threaten the very viability of Mexico as a sovereign democracy. This is the nature of the threat that we are facing.

The last time we had comprehensive immigration reform in this country was in 1986 with the passage of the Immigration Reform and Control Act. This legislation gave amnesty to any illegal immigrants who had arrived before 1982, and it is responsible for the tidal wave of illegal immigrants that we saw in the '90s.

When the Senate was considering immigration reform 3 years ago, many warned about what had happened after 1986. The administration, in particular former Arizona Governor Janet Napolitano who was then Secretary of Homeland Security, promised the American people that it would be different this time because the border was secure. If a wave of illegal immigrants came, Border Patrol would handle it. It was a terrific talking point. Too bad it was completely untrue and ignored the emergence of the Mexican drug cartels.

Although immigration reform is a distant memory, the administration is painted into a corner now. If the border is secure, how do you ask Congress for more manpower? If the border is secure, how do you ask for money for additional air support, for technology, and for more fencing?

For the administration, the answer is real simple: You don't. You don't talk about the Mexican drug cartels. You talk about how apprehensions are down and how well things are going. If we are going to get serious and solve this problem, we first have to be honest and admit that a problem does exist.

If you are serious about confronting the drug cartels, there are some concrete steps that need to be taken.

First, manpower. The National Border Patrol Council believes the Border Patrol is at least 5,000 agents below where we need to be to be effectively controlling the border.

More agents in the field. The Border Patrol is an extremely top-heavy organization, with multiple layers of management that are completely removed from the field. If the Border Patrol has the same supervisory staffing ratio that Sheriff Dannels' department has, we could return close to 2,000 agents back to the field.

More effective deployment. Currently, almost all of our resources are clustered too close to the border. We are effectively playing goal line defense every single day. If an illegal immigrant or drug smuggler gets more than 10 miles north of the border, they will likely not be caught. We need to have a defense-in-depth with multiple layers in order to be effective. We also need to make rational decisions on the use of forward operating bases. Forward operating bases had a time and place years ago but are an incredibly inefficient use of resources today.

End our catch-and-release program. One of the main drivers of illegal immigration is our own immigration policy. For example, under the current policy, if a Border Patrol Agent does not physically see an illegal immigrant cross the border and the illegal immigrant claims they have been here since 2014, we have been ordered to process them and let them go. In many instances, we will be letting them go without even issuing a Notice to Appear. This is a policy that is senseless and is literally driving illegal immigration to our front door.

I want to thank you for giving me the opportunity to testify, and I am happy to answer any questions that you may have.

[The prepared statement of Mr. Del Cueto follows:]

PREPARED STATEMENT OF ART DEL CUETO

MAY 9, 2016

Chairwoman McSally and Ranking Member Vela, thank you for providing me the opportunity to testify on behalf of the National Border Patrol Council (NBPC).

The NBPC represents the interests of 16,500 Line Agents at the Border Patrol and my name is Art Del Cueto. I am a native of Douglas, Arizona and have been with the Border Patrol since 2003.

CURRENT SITUATION AT THE BORDER

One of the many areas in which the Border Patrol excels is keeping statistics. Border Patrol can tell you in detail how many agents we have, the number of overtime hours worked, the number of apprehensions, or hours of air support delivered by CBP air and marine operations. It's really quite impressive. If I was a Member of Congress from a non-border State and I sat through a CBP briefing about how the border was secure I would be inclined to believe them.

The primary statistic that Commissioner Kerlikowske talks about today, in support of his assertion that the border is secure, is the number of apprehensions, which is down. At the height of illegal immigration in 2000, Border Patrol apprehended 1.6 million people. In the Tucson sector alone that year, we arrested 616,000 illegal immigrants. To put this in perspective, the entire population of Tucson in 2000 was 486,000. That was how massive the influx was.

Back in 2000, we were facing a wave of Mexican economic migrants in search of employment. There was little organization and most illegal immigrants simply loaded up a backpack of supplies, jumped the border and headed north. This lack of organization frankly made them relatively easy to catch if you could deploy Border Patrol manpower.

Fast forward to 2016 and the entire border is controlled by Mexican drug cartels. The drug cartels control the border in the same way that most prisons are controlled by the inmates. Nothing moves along this border without their permission and illegal aliens and narcotics are simply 2 lines of business within the same organization.

Here in Arizona, we have the Sinaloa Cartel. The 63,000 individuals we arrested last year in this sector paid the cartel a considerable amount of money to cross. Only based on the individuals we arrested in this sector, the Sinaloa Cartel made millions from illegal alien smuggling.

If there is one point that I want to make in this entire testimony it is that the money that the cartels earn from illegal alien smuggling underwrites the same organizations that are flooding our streets with narcotics. Money is flowing back to the same organizations that are responsible for the violence in Mexico which has murdered over 150,000 people. It is going back to the same organizations that threaten the very viability of Mexico as a sovereign democracy. This is the nature of the threat we are facing.

FAILURE TO ADMIT THERE IS A PROBLEM

The last time we had comprehensive immigration reform in this country was 1986 with the passage of the Immigration Reform and Control Act. This legislation gave amnesty to any illegal immigrant who had arrived before 1982 and is responsible for the tidal wave of illegal immigrants we saw in the 1990s.

When the Senate was considering immigration reform 3 years ago, many warned about what happened after 1986. The administration, in particular, former Arizona Governor Janet Napolitano who was then Secretary of Homeland Security, promised the American people that it would be different this time because the border was secure. If a wave of illegal immigrants came Border Patrol would handle it. It was a terrific talking point. Too bad it was completely untrue and ignored the emergence of the Mexican drug cartels.

Although immigration reform is a distant memory, the administration is painted into a corner. If the border is secure, how do you ask Congress for more manpower? If the border is secure, how do you ask for money for additional air support, technology, and fencing?

For the administration, the answer is that you don't. You do not talk about the Mexican drug cartels. You talk about how apprehensions are down and how well things are going. If we are going to get serious and solve this problem we first have to have the honesty to admit that a problem exists.

SOLUTIONS

If you are serious about confronting the Mexican drug cartels there are some concrete steps that can be taken:

More manpower.—The NBPC believes the Border Patrol is at least 5,000 agents below where we need to be to effectively control the border.

More agents in the field.—Border Patrol is an extremely top-heavy organization with multiple layers of management that are completely removed from the field. If the Border Patrol has the same supervisory staffing ratio that Sheriff Dannels' department has, we could return another 2,000 line agents to the field.

More effective deployment.—Currently almost all of our resources are clustered too close to the border. We are effectively playing goal line defense every single day and if an illegal immigrant or drug smuggler gets more than 10 miles north of the border they will likely not be caught. We need to have a defense-in-depth with multiple layers in order to be effective. We also need to make rational decisions on the use of Forward Operating Bases (FOB). FOBs had a time and place years ago but are an incredibly inefficient use of resources today.

End our catch-and-release policy—One of the main drivers of illegal immigration is our own immigration policy. For example, under current policy, if a Border Patrol Agent does not physically see an illegal immigrant cross the border and the illegal immigrant claims they have been here since 2014, we have been ordered to process them and let them go. In many instances, we will let them go without even issuing a Notice to Appear. This is policy is senseless and is literally driving illegal immigration to our front door.

I want to thank you for giving me the opportunity to testify and I am happy to answer any questions that you might have.

Ms. McSALLY. Thanks, Mr. Del Cueto.

I now recognize myself for some opening questions, and then I will provide opportunities for Mr. Pearce, and then we will probably have a couple of rounds here.

First I want to ask really the whole panel a 2-part question. The first one is, what do you think is the biggest misperception in Washington, DC on what is really going on in the border? The second part of that is in a little over 8 months we are going to have a new Commander-in-Chief. We are going to have a new Secretary of Homeland Security. If you were asked—you are the new Secretary or you were asked by the new Secretary what is it that we need to do in order to secure the border, you were resource-unconstrained, what would your answer be to that question?

I will start with Sheriff Dannels.

Sheriff DANNELS. Thank you. The first thing is take off the myth. Mr. Del Cueto states it clearly. You have to identify there is a problem, and that has been a myth through media, through different chains, different avenues. But the bottom line is they need to identify there is a problem so you can fix the problem, and that the border is not secure. This plan needs redefinition, like I said in my brief, in my verbal statement today. We have to identify that.

No. 2 is you have all layers of Government working together, starting at the local. Community problems have been addressed for years and years, have been successfully addressed in communities first, not in Washington, DC. You have to start with your local law enforcement, your citizens that live it and breathe it, along with our State partners, and then our Federal partners. That is why we take the oath of office. That is why we are leaders, to work together in partnership.

Ms. McSALLY. Thanks, Sheriff Dannels.

Mayor Ortega.

Mr. ORTEGA. I guess I have a little different perspective. I think our border communities are very safe on both sides of the border.

The sister cities Agua Prieta and Douglas are very safe communities, and there is a lot of trade that goes back and forth between our communities.

Unfortunately, I disagree with Mr. Del Cueto. I think, in talking to some of the outlying areas, they want more agents closer to the border to try to stop the people illegally coming across, primarily drugs at this time. But as far as our community goes, our community is safe, but I think the outlying areas are not, and I think they would like to see more agents closer to the border.

I wish there were some incentives to have the Border Patrol actually live within our communities. It seems as though we don't have agents living within our communities, getting to know who we are as a community, who the good people and who the bad people are. I think that would ease a lot of the relations between the Border Patrol and the communities that they serve.

Ms. McSALLY. Okay. Thanks, Mayor Ortega.

Mr. Del Cueto.

Mr. DEL CUETO. I would outline what I have stated previous. The border is not secure. There are many communities within Mexico where the drug cartels and the people who work for these cartels run rampant. Just in the sister city of Douglas, I believe a year ago they declared some kind of law where they had to close down the streets at 10:00 p.m. because people were getting randomly murdered. I think we need to pay attention to the boots on the ground and get away from this dog-and-pony show that the District of Columbia brings down here to the border and explains that everything is nice and happy. It is not. It is a war zone out there.

In the Tucson sector alone, I believe within these last 2 weeks we have had 3 shootings already. It is not secure. There are individuals that, once they get past the agents that are near the border, they pretty much are home free and it is harder for us to find them and detect them.

Thank you.

Ms. McSALLY. Great. Thank you.

So, I don't want to put words in anybody's mouth, but do all of you agree that—and again, I think this is the second-order consequences of the strategy over the years, right? It has been populated areas first. Again, we saw in California addressing it and then pushing the activity into Arizona, and then within Arizona addressing trying to deal with the urban areas first, pushing the illegal activities into the rural areas.

So the consequence of that is the rural areas is where the high propensity of this, especially cartel activity, is happening, which is increasing danger and security for those who are living out in the rural areas. Is that a fair statement to make that the whole panel agrees upon?

Sheriff DANNELS. I would agree.

If I could say something, Mayor Ortega, when he speaks about the security of his city, he is a direct product of that plan from the '90s, and he is exactly right. Douglas is safer than it ever has been, but that illegal activity, as you are describing, is in Cochise County in the rural parts, and those folks who live out there don't deserve that.

Ms. McSALLY. Do you agree?

Mr. ORTEGA. Yes, I do.

Mr. DEL CUETO. Yes.

Ms. MCSALLY. Okay, thank you. So given that now we are dealing with a public safety issue to these rural communities that are often miles and miles away from another individual, out there kind-of on their own dealing with this cartel activity, what do we do to change that? We have differences of opinion on at the border/ away from the border. We can continue to talk about that. But what about the combination of barriers, technology, air assets, manpower? Does anybody have a comment on the strategy as it relates to the mix of these types of tools and where there needs to be a change, a new strategy, more resources related to the types of tools that are not just the number of agents and where the agents are but the larger strategy? I just want to hear from everybody on that.

Sheriff DANNELS. I can start with that. You know, there was a bill that was attempted to be passed several years ago. The Gang of Eight wanted to add 20,000 more agents, and I know the Southwest Border Sheriffs, the Arizona Sheriffs Association, we took a large stand on that because there was no strategic plan to place those 20,000 agents. Show me a business that can hire 20,000 more employees and not have a plan.

I think we need to take an assessment of the current plan, put that forward. As you said, 5,000 more agents, whatever the number is, but strategically know what you are going to do with those agents, and bring that plan back to the border where you know the problem is beginning, not downtown Phoenix but at the border, and then take it backwards from there.

The other thing is, and I think it is something that needs to be said, is what does get through that border is not just Cochise County's problem. It is America's problem. The heroin is coming through, as we know. I have testified on that before. The methamphetamine, the marijuana that goes into these communities throughout the United States is an epidemic. There is a cultural mindset that needs to be educated, that needs prevention. The fact is that if we don't change our social ways, our cultural ways, because the United States folks here have a healthy appetite for those drugs, if we didn't have that appetite, we wouldn't have the demand and they wouldn't be able to ship it across. We need to take a real hard look at that and take a comprehensive look at how we are doing business, and listen to the line agents. They know.

I teach at one of the universities. I hear in my classes the frustration that they see it, they live it, they breathe it too. They have to have a voice at this table beside somebody who doesn't work the border, is disconnected. We have to have that voice there.

Then you have the economic side, like the mayor is addressing today. I took an oath for public safety, not for economics. That is my oath of office is to protect my citizens. As he is looking for legal trade, legal immigration, I have no issue with it. It is the illegal aspect I am after.

Ms. MCSALLY. Mayor Ortega.

Mr. ORTEGA. I also think we need some investment in not only the infrastructure of our ports but the technology within our ports. As you have seen, our areas are very rugged. It would be hard to get a vehicle in there, even with roads. I have heard from some ranchers that when you build a road, you build a road also for illegal drug traffic to come across. I think we need to be careful with that one.

But there is technology out there, whether it is drones or that type of equipment, to survey the outlying areas, but also the increased technology at our ports of entry. I think we are going to start seeing more drug trade crossing through our ports unless we invest in some infrastructure to check not only the trucks but the passenger vehicles as well.

Ms. McSally. Thanks.

Mr. Del Cueto.

Mr. DEL CUETO. One of the big things we need to focus on is these policies. We need to change and start enforcing some of these policies that we have on the books. Currently, like other people have noted, the illegal immigrants that enter in Arizona, the numbers have gone down. But like I stated earlier, those numbers have gone down because the drug cartels are the ones that are running everything on the south side.

The Tucson sector currently still sits well over 50 percent of all the drug seizures in the entire country. That is an outstanding number. We need to take care of that.

What I mean by some of these policies is, first of all, the catch-and-release program that has been so much talked about. There is no disincentive for Central Americans currently to enter the United States. Currently we can have a group, a family—and I am going to give you an example. You can have a family of people from Central America that come. They turn themselves in, which is what is happening in Texas. The numbers in Texas are going up because they are turning themselves in. We are not catching these individuals.

So we have these Central Americans who are turning themselves in. They come to the Border Patrol, we take them into our facilities. We do the proper checks to see if they have any prior criminal history within the United States, but we are not aware of any history that they might have in Central America. So what happens with these individuals is they are turned over to ICE, and ICE then releases them into our communities. They are going to all different parts of the United States. They tell them that they have to come back and report to an immigration office. These people are never reporting back to the immigration office.

So what we have done with these policies is we have facilitated an open door for these Central Americans, and we have no idea what crimes they have committed in their country. We have no idea if they can be rapists, murderers, ax murderers. We just don't know who these people are, and we have facilitated a way for them to remain in this country. They have ties with who knows who back in Central America.

That is where we need to start, with these policies that are on the books that are being pushed. They need to stop. We don't know how many people they have released. I think that is a number that should be asked of ICE. We don't know how many of these Central Americans with possible criminal backgrounds in their own country that we have no idea where they are at.

Ms. MCSALLY. Okay, thanks.

Back to those who are trying to evade, the cartels that are bringing drugs across the border, I want to hear your comments on, do we need additional barriers, additional technology or assets? You have mentioned the agents, but what else do you think would address those who are trying to evade you?

Mr. DEL CUETO. You hear so much talk publicly about this wall, and some people say the wall works, some people say that the wall doesn't work. Well, it is not just the wall that we need. Obviously, a wall is a huge deterrent. We would see how it was back in the mid-'90s in the Douglas area alone, where it was easier to cross the border because there was less of a wall there, less of a barrier. The barrier works.

We need, obviously, more agents on the ground. We need agents to be able to move back and forth, not just stay on the border, on the line itself.

We do need more technology.

We need more vehicles. The vehicles get treated really rough at times, but it is because that is just the nature of the job. We definitely need more vehicles.

There is just a lot of different things that we would need, vehicles, night vision goggles, sensors. It is a mass amount that we need out there.

Ms. MCSALLY. Okay, great. Thank you.

Mr. Pearce.

Mr. PEARCE. Thank you very much. I appreciate all of your testimony.

Mr. Del Cueto, I really appreciate the straightforwardness. That is something that I think we in Washington hunger for. But when you talk to those people up the chains of command, frankly, it gets muddled, and outright untruths are told. So having you sit here and tell the truth as you see it from the ground level is extremely valuable.

I am going to come back with some hardball questions in a minute for you, but they are not directed at you. It is the decisions made somewhere above you and, frankly, I can't get answers. So I will come back, but don't take them personally because I really do appreciate that you are saying things that we all believe, that the cartels own the border. That is very powerful for someone inside an agency to say that, the agency that is charged with it.

Mr. Ortega, I want to do a little housekeeping on you. You were saying that you would disagree with the other two, that the border is secure and that you feel safe. Now, when the Sheriff said, well, the city is safe but it is not in the rural areas, you are shaking your head.

The headshakes don't show up in the transcript, frankly. So in Washington, they are going to quote you, "No, this man says it is okay." So could you confirm just verbally that you would agree that the rural areas are struggling for feeling safe while your area feels okay as it is?

Mr. DEL CUETO. Yes, sir, that is correct.

Mr. PEARCE. Okay. All right. So we got you on the record. Because people will take your one sentence and that will be the only thing they will extract out of this entire hearing. So again, I appreciate the recognition.

Now, Mr. Del Cueto, you say that you would use 5,000 more people. I was there—and keep in mind that we had to fight the Bush administration equally as hard as this one. It is not a Republican/Democrat issue. It is Washington saying everything is okay and we are going to do it this way, and the people out in the field are going to say they are lying or cheating or stealing or something.

So I watched as we put 10,000 more agents—we doubled the patrol, from 10,000-something, 12,000, up to about 23,000. Yet, the general consensus of people who live on the Mexico side of the border said it didn't change things a bit.

Tell me how 5,000 people would solve that or why that 10,000 didn't, if you can. Again, I know this should be coming from way high up, but they just refuse to answer the question, frankly, in the hearings up there.

Mr. DEL CUETO. So, it is a 2-part question. I will first start with the mass amounts of hirings that we did, with the extra 10,000 that you mentioned. A lot of this issue is the Border Patrol grew but other agencies didn't grow. So what happened many times is these same agents that we hired within the Patrol were farmed out to other agencies. There were agents farmed out to prosecutions within the States. There were also agents that were farmed out to the ports of entry. Some of our canines were sent to the ports of entry. So a lot of the new agents that came in were farmed out to other agencies, and at the same time they developed other programs. So I believe that is where the top-heaviness comes in. They put too many agents in other programs that aren't really line agents.

So when we ask for these additional 5,000 agents, that is why it is a mixture of the policies and the internal business within the Border Patrol where they need to know how to deploy these agents and do away with some of these programs and maybe some of these top-heavy agency programs that we do have.

Mr. PEARCE. Okay. Now, from your testimony—and you don't have to answer the next question. Feel free to just say, hey, I am not touching that. But from your testimony, it seems that you were critical of the amnesty program back under Reagan because we did not do anything to secure the border. So my question is—and keep in mind that Washington, from our side of the table, only talks big issues. They don't ever get down and really discuss what we are discussing here today.

So amnesty versus not amnesty. Is amnesty productive, or is it simply an encouragement of other people, that if I get there illegally, they will fix it? You don't have to answer if you don't want to.

Mr. DEL CUETO. To help you out, you did tell me I didn't have to answer it, but unfortunately I am going to go ahead and answer it.

Mr. PEARCE. Nice.

Mr. DEL CUETO. It does not help. I lived in Douglas, like I said before, and I saw many people that would cross into Douglas that never lived here, that never worked here, and they would pay different business owners not just in Douglas I would say, but business owners within the United States so they can get paperwork stating that they had been here, and then those individuals, a lot of them were able to obtain amnesty. Some of the individuals that were actually here and fit in the mold for the amnesty program never did because they couldn't get the $5,000 to whoever employed them at that point to give them documentation.

Mr. PEARCE. So in your estimation, the great resource from the cartels came from drug smuggling. Now it sounds like human smuggling probably eclipses that and drugs are a secondary revenue producer. What is your opinion of that?

Mr. DEL CUETO. Well, I think it is both. Like I said, through intel that we acquire when we catch different individuals in these areas, the Border Patrol has received information and we know that a lot of these individuals, they run the drug smuggling and the people smuggling.

So, yes, the drugs are the ones that are making most of the money.

Mr. PEARCE. The next question is not meant to trick you. I will come over to you, Sheriff. But it is intended instead, I think, to reflect the culture that ties the hands of our Border Patrol Agents. I have sat out there on the border in the night. I think that our agents could and would do the deal, but I think people above them give them policies like the catch-and-release policy. So again, these are not very easy questions. You can dodge it if you want to.

I read somewhere that there are approximately 1,300 Border Patrol Agents in Cochise County, more or less?

Sheriff DANNELS. That is correct.

Mr. PEARCE. That is correct.

Sheriff DANNELS. We have 1,300 Border Patrol Agents——

Mr. PEARCE. I didn't get to my question yet. You were going to take the easy road. I am not going to let you. Excuse me.

[Laughter.]

Mr. PEARCE. If you had 1,300 people under your command, could you secure the border there in Cochise County?

Sheriff DANNELS. Yes.

Mr. PEARCE. All right. So just to repeat what we did, because you are getting counseled there—that's good. It is trying to protect us all. I will probably need counsel at this stage myself.

But what I ask is if he could secure the border with 1,300 people, and he says yes. Now, I tend to agree that if—and it is not your people. Again, it is the process and it is the system. If you had your 1,300 people and we turned you loose and said secure the border, I think you could. I don't know that the process, I don't know that the system is ever going to let you do it.

So many times I say the only solution is to take the resources and let them work for local elected law officials. Right now, local citizens have no recourse at all. They get frustrated. They get angry. They speak to people like us. They get us stirred up. We come out and we make you all angry, and it is because nobody is accountable.

I sincerely believe because, again, I have been on the border with the agents out there with their boots on the ground, and I know the heart they have to do it, and they talk the same way that you talk here today. So I have a great appreciation and a great love I have for those agents is dispelled because the system is plain keeping it from working. So always I just say if a local sheriff had the responsibility and he had your resources, he could do it, and if he didn't, they could un-elect him. But right now, the system cannot respond. So somewhere a solution has to reach that level.

A couple more questions on process, Mr. Del Cueto. So I have heard—I don't know if it is just scuttlebutt or whatever—that if people are headed south, if the footprints are headed south, somebody that has created a crime, they just don't pursue them because they are headed south and they are probably going to get there before we get them. That is something we hear a lot in New Mexico. Maybe it is true, maybe it is not. Maybe it is just those guys over in El Paso.

Mr. DEL CUETO. I can't testify to that one. I can tell you that here, I myself work the field and I have followed footprints all the way south. Some of the issues that we have is we don't know how many are in the footprint. So what you do is you chase a group, whether it be headed north or be headed south, and these individuals walk in a line. So if you can count 5 footprints, you would say 5 to 10 people.

I remember chasing a group where I counted 15 footprints, and I called back and I said we have 20-plus. We continued chasing this group, and when we finally apprehended it, it was a group of 60 people. So when you are saying 20 plus 60, that is a big difference between 20-plus. Most people say 20-plus and it is 23, 24 people. In this instance it was 60 individuals, and that is a huge deal.

To touch back on having more agents and Mr. Dannels said that he could control it with 1,300 agents, a lot of the thing is some of these agents are put in VCO positions, so they need to take care of the vehicles. A lot of these agents are put in processing; they need to process. We have different agents that are detailed to different positions.

I will state down in Cochise County there are agents that, before we used to work on different areas of the border—I understand the ranchers' concerns. I understand that there are ranchers who need more agents in their area. So what that has caused, it has caused a lot of the agents to not work certain areas, and you have some agents bunched up near the ranchers. So now what has happened is you have left other areas more porous.

It was just recently in the news, in Cochise County alone 2 vehicles came through. We never apprehended those vehicles. We don't know what was in those vehicles. We don't know where those vehicles are. At that point it was limited resources that were available in that area. The majority of these agents were stationed over near the ranchers.

Mr. PEARCE. Okay. I just have 1 follow-up to that and I will put you back. If you go to a second round, I will obviously have a couple more questions here.

So the idea has also been pitched out in New Mexico and local sheriffs have said it is true, I don't know that it is true, but the idea that Border Patrol just doesn't seek out or prosecute or hold people with less than a certain amount of drugs, and that number usually varies somewhere between 120 and 150 pounds, maybe more. Is that the thing that you find in your directives, or is that something you don't want to comment on? Again, feel free not to comment. I am not trying to do anything to your career.

Mr. DEL CUETO. Well, I have been doing this for quite some time, so I think my career and moving up in the Border Patrol is pretty much shot already.

Mr. PEARCE. It sounds like we both started the same.

[Laughter.]

Mr. DEL CUETO. I appreciate you putting the nail in the coffin on this one.

[Laughter.]

Mr. PEARCE. No sweat.

Mr. DEL CUETO. There is many times when we do arrest individuals, and we do call the prosecutor, and the prosecutor says it fails to meet prosecution guidelines. I will say that.

Mr. PEARCE. All right.

Madam Chairwoman, thank you very much. I appreciate this. This is very good information, and I yield back.

Ms. McSALLY. Great, thanks.

Okay, we are going to do another round here.

Sheriff Dannels, it was in your written testimony. I want to allow you an opportunity to elaborate on the use of spotters; and, actually, Mr. Del Cueto as well. This is something we have heard from the community, from multiple law enforcement agencies, that the cartels are using spotters on hilltops with often better communications than our guys have, encrypted, solar panels, and sometimes they are up there for 30 days at a time. If we can get them, it is very difficult to prosecute them because you can't connect them to a specific drug load, and so they are often just processed as somebody who is just here illegally.

This was brought to our attention. We actually introduced a bill related to spotter activity, simply making it a Federal crime to be a spotter, and aiding and abetting cartel operations in this way. So I just want to highlight your thoughts, and also Mr. Del Cueto, on the trends that you have seen related to spotters.

Sheriff DANNELS. Representative McSally, you are exactly right. When it comes to catching them, that is the biggest obstacle. Our helicopter sees them up on the top of the mountains. It is very difficult to see them. When you do see them, just catch them is the other half of it. They run off and it is very, very hard to catch them. I have one rancher down there that actually has a camera that looks onto the Mexico side. It is a border ranch. There is a house on top of the mountain, and that scouter watches everything on that Southwest Border in that area and directs that traffic around. We watch them all the time with that camera.

But we know they are in Cochise. Our ranch patrol deputies ride their horses, ride right up on them, and they run, and we get them. It is tough, very tough. I will say this, though, as a solution-based thought, that our new border team that was put together, in the first 2 years they had 400 apprehensions. This is a team of about 4 Border Patrol Agents and about 4 deputies that work part-time that have been tremendous in their efforts to get these smugglers, to get these scouts off these mountains, out of these ranchlands. So, 400. About half of that was just pure illegals that were turned over to Border Patrol. The other half were smugglers, burglar suspects, had broke into homes, you name it. We have 100 percent prosecution at the State level.

One thing that we did here a few months ago, the county attorney and I, we sat down with Arizona's attorney general and said you have to step up the game here, you have to help us. I mean, our juvenile prosecutions are financially hurting us, straining us. The answer was I can't, there are no teeth in the law on the Federal side, which obviously puts the burden back onto local, where there is no financial support for that.

But it is the right thing to do. In the last few months I believe it has been, we have had 51 go through my jail, juvenile backpackers. That is sad, it is very sad, but it is real in our county. I know Yuma County, Pima, Santa Cruz, they are dealing with the same thing I am. That is where the local government has to be supported.

Or the other thing we were talking about with the Arizona attorney was you have to hire more prosecutors. I mean, you can't put just the enforcement component, support that and not the jails, the defense, the prosecution. It all has to be a balanced approach in the criminal justice system, and then the education and prevention side of it too.

Ms. MCSALLY. Thank you.

Mr. Del Cueto.

Mr. DEL CUETO. Can you repeat the question, please?

Ms. MCSALLY. Yes, sure, related to scouts and spotters, are you seeing any trends?

Mr. DEL CUETO. Yes. Working this job since 2003, I would like to use examples. I am going to give you an example. Approximately 3 years ago we apprehended a few individuals, and they had 1,600 pounds of marijuana. When we apprehended these individuals, they were about 20 miles into the United States. We debriefed, we spoke to them, and they did admit that there was close to 15 different spotters along that area. So in a 20-mile span, there were 15 different spotters. I think 1 spotter is too many. Fifteen spotters? That is just ridiculous.

These spotters, they do stay up there for months at a time. They have different individuals both from the Mexican side and citizens of this country that go up these hills, and they provide them with food, they provide them with drugs, and we have information that at times they even provide them with women who go up there and take care of them while they are waiting for the drugs to come through. That is just amazing, and I think it is unacceptable as a Border Patrol Agent. It is unacceptable as a union leader for the agents that I represent, and frankly it should be unacceptable by any citizen of this country.

Ms. MCSALLY. Are you guys told not to go when you know they are up there, not to go up there and get them? Or when you get them, your hands are tied as to what to do with them?

Mr. DEL CUETO. It is just hard to determine where they are at. That is the problem. It is hard to determine exactly where they are at. Many times when we go to these areas, by the time we hump up the hill, they hear us coming and they are humping down the other side. So it is cat and mouse every day.

Ms. McSALLY. It sounds like a little air support may be helpful for situational awareness during operations like that.

Mr. DEL CUETO. That would be nice. We understand it is limited on air support in certain areas also. We need a lot of help out there.

Ms. McSALLY. Thanks.

I want to get everybody's opinions on interior checkpoints. I know there are going to be differences of opinion within this panel and with the next panel, but I want to give everybody the opportunity to share their perspectives on how those impact the security operations or any other impacts related to your roles.

Sheriff Dannels.

Sheriff DANNELS. Well, it has become a cultural norm in our county to have to go through a checkpoint and claim your citizenship as an American, and I hear that all the time from the citizens, how that is. Though it is real to us, it may not be real to downtown Maricopa County or other parts of this country. It is real to us.

The other thing to a local sheriff that is important is the fact that every time you establish an international port away from the border—I will give you an example, the Wet Stone area, which is north of Sierra Vista. That is the international port of Wet Stone. What happens is the smugglers know when the checkpoint is open based on scouting reports. When it is open, they drop their smuggling product, whether it be humans or dope, and they go around the checkpoint into these communities, and guess who gets called on? We do. Again, another burden on us, and it is tough for us. We work closely with the Border Patrol trying to get out there. We have air support that helps us. But again, it is tough, challenging.

The biggest complaint I hear is that since the border is not secure in the rural parts, and then we have secondary checkpoints, it is kind of counterproductive. The primary focus should be on the border. Once that is secured to a point where the stakeholders are satisfied—I don't know if it will ever be perfect. I have never seen perfect on our border. I don't know if it ever will be. But then we can work on secondary.

So it is a big challenge, a lot of complaints on it, to be honest with you.

Ms. McSALLY. Mayor Ortega.

Mr. ORTEGA. I agree with Sheriff Dannels. First, they are not open 24/7. If it is raining or if sometimes the weather is inclement, they close the checkpoints. But it does put a burden on the communities surrounding the checkpoints. So I agree with Sheriff Dannels, and I would rather see the agents closer to the border and stopping the problems at the border, versus 25 or 40 miles out.

Ms. McSALLY. Mr. Del Cueto.

Mr. DEL CUETO. If members of this panel and different members of law enforcement have said before that they do not believe that the border will ever be secure, and you bring all the agents down to the border, if this border is never going to be secure, what do you do with the people who do go around us? That is why these checkpoints are important. You want to sacrifice having a checkpoint in these communities, send all the agents to the border. What happens if something gets through us? What happens when they go through these roads, through these main roads down on 90, on the main roads over here off of Wilcox and the Tombstone area, Nogales? They serve a purpose. They serve a good purpose. They help derail. They help deter some of the traffic that comes through. There was a time when we would see an astronomical amount of vehicles up on I–10 headed towards Phoenix. They serve a purpose.

Ms. McSALLY. I would like to follow up on that, and then I will hand it over to Mr. Pearce. My understanding from talking to individuals within Border Patrol and the community, this defense-in-depth, which includes the interior checkpoints in both of our districts, because you have them in New Mexico as well, was based originally on the strategy of pushing the activity into the rural areas, like we talked about, but then not having enough resources to be able to really intercept it very quickly. With limited resources, the best way to address that is to figure out how to funnel the illegal activity into a place that we can monitor and intercept at a time and place of our choosing. That is the way the strategy has been described to me.

I may not be parroting it back perfectly, but I have heard again from individuals from leadership positions in CBP that they feel they have seconds to minutes to intercept activity in urban areas, and they say hours to days to intercept it in rural areas. So therefore this defense-in-depth strategy, which includes the interior checkpoints, what was described to me is that the primary role of the interior checkpoints is to make the cartels go around them. I mean, the low-level criminals and others are going to get the Darwin award by coming through a known law enforcement checkpoint with drugs, which I still don't totally understand. But those who are actually the serious traffickers are going to go around, which then again pushes the activity into maybe more difficult terrain, which might be easier for you all to corner them.

The challenge with all that that we will hear—we have heard from some of this panel, and we will hear from the second panel. I know we won't have the interaction, but that all might sound reasonable if we didn't have people living in those areas between where they cross and where you can eventually intercept them, 50 or 100 miles inland. So it is that public safety threat to those that are living in those areas that are then having the traffic funneled into them which is the main point of feedback that I am getting really across the board.

So I guess I hear what you are saying, that if you don't have enough resources, that maybe you do need to fall back and have—sorry to use the football analogy you all hate, but everybody is playing safety instead of being at the line of scrimmage. But if you had the resources that you needed, if we were using intelligence-driven operations, if we were detecting the cartel activity and knowing their lines of activity, and being nimble, because as soon as you squeeze them they move somewhere else, they become much more nimble than we are generally because we are more bureaucratic.

So if you had all those resources and you had the ability, the vehicles, the ATVs, the horses, the air assets to be able to quickly intercept them right at the border, would you then agree—I am not trying to get you to agree, but I am trying to find areas of common ground. If we had the resources, would you agree that it is better to intercept them at the border with maybe a couple of safeties, as opposed to our fallback, where we are right now, which is based on a lack of resources? Can you understand the concerns that we have as law enforcement in the community that the public safety challenge happens because of all that space is ceded, and that is what creates the threats to individuals in our community, if we are focused on intercepting so far inland?

Mr. DEL CUETO. I agree with what you say, but I think one of the big things that you did say is you still need the safety to catch that pass, and that is the big deal.

Ms. MCSALLY. A couple of them. I think you have 2 on a team, right?

Mr. DEL CUETO. You still need those.

Ms. MCSALLY. Right.

Mr. DEL CUETO. I mean, honestly, that is what you still need.

Ms. MCSALLY. Okay. Would you consider the checkpoints to be those if we had the resources to intercept quickly and have you guys be able to nimbly intercept at the border? Would you still think we would need these interior checkpoints?

Mr. DEL CUETO. Yes, because things are still going to get through, and these checkpoints help with a lot of that. We have noticed that with the checkpoints there, our apprehensions have helped considerably in those areas. Yes, they move to more rural areas, but the agents are out there to intercept those spots. I mean, pretty much what we are saying is if we get enough people at the border, then we don't need the checkpoints. But we are still going to have things that go through. So if you were to tell me get rid of some of these checkpoints, first and foremost, it is not up to me to get rid of. Second of all, we still need some of these checkpoints.

So I am not going to sit here and agree we need to get rid of them. We still need some of them. Which ones they are, that would be up to the agency to decide on that. But I can tell you that some of the issues we have at these checkpoints, as I understand it, the people that live in these areas are fed up with the checkpoints. A lot of times when they come through these checkpoints it would make it so much easier both on them and on the agent. It is a simple "Are you a United States citizen?" "Yes, I am." "Have a good day." A lot of times they will refuse to roll down their window, they will get confrontational with the agent, there is a lot of back and forth.

These agents, like we said earlier, they live within the communities too. These agents are just out there doing their job, and that is what a lot of the people need to understand. They are not here to give anyone a hard time. They are here to do their job, that is it. They are here to protect our borders. They are here to make sure that whatever gets through the border is properly intercepted, it is properly screened, and that our communities are not just safer along the border but throughout the United States. That is the agents' job at these checkpoints.

Ms. MCSALLY. Thanks.

Mr. Pearce.

Mr. PEARCE. Thank you.

I thought I was going to move off of Mr. Del Cueto, but no such luck, because you are saying such stimulating things. I might listen or might not listen to the words you are saying because, frankly, I had a much different opinion about the interior checkpoints. But I can hear the passion and the intensity, and when I see someone who has established the credibility here today that you have established with this group, then I pay attention when people are invested in something. So we might not agree on it, but we would sit at the table if it were just this group trying to solve the problem.

I am going to switch over to the sheriff. So people who want to push the argument that the border is secure, and there are a lot in Washington who want to push that, I have a simple question: Is the price of drugs going up dramatically on the street? Because really, drugs are like everything else. They are a commodity, and if the supply is being squeezed off as dramatically as is being talked about in Washington, then the price would be skyrocketing. So are you seeing a skyrocketing price in drugs?

Sheriff DANNELS. Or not. Actually with heroin, it has actually gone down.

Mr. PEARCE. So there is too much supply. It is coming in too readily and the price is going down.

Sheriff DANNELS. Correct.

Mr. PEARCE. Now, the access through public lands is, again, a heated debate. The President just drew an Executive Order declaring much of the border area and New Mexico as a monument, wilderness, whatever. They are all the same. Is the Organ Pipe National Monument, has that still got the signs up there requesting people not to go in there, American citizens, saying you should not go in there because it is too dangerous?

Sheriff DANNELS. I haven't been on that.

Mr. PEARCE. Mr. Del Cueto, do you happen to know that? So we are getting a head shake out from the audience. Are these guys respectable behind you? I am just joking, but I am getting head shakes out there.

Mr. DEL CUETO. I don't know who those people are.

Mr. PEARCE. Okay. You are not identifying them, and they can't identify you at this stage.

Mr. DEL CUETO. I don't know if it is still there yet. I mean, I honestly don't know.

Mr. PEARCE. But the idea is it is still very dangerous in the Organ Pipes.

Mr. DEL CUETO. Correct. Somebody forgot to tell the drug smugglers and the illegal aliens that you are not supposed to walk on that land.

Mr. PEARCE. Yes, they can't get on the wilderness area.

When I was the Chair of the Subcommittee on National Parks, we toured a lot of these. When we went out to the redwood forest, whatever that is out there, they actually are planting marijuana back in the forest, in the Sequoia National Forest so far that they just tell backpackers that you can't go beyond here because you are going to hit a tripwire and the shotgun they have laying out there on the trail is going to blow your head off. So they actually stop the traffic because we grow so much marijuana in our National forest that the law enforcement officers can't get there. You, Sheriff, you don't have free access to chase people who are doing illegal stuff. You have to go through some bureaucratic process to go in and check illegal activity.

Sheriff DANNELS. Well, in our forest lands, we don't ask. If there is a crime, we go, we go, whether it be an accident, whether it be a search-and-rescue.

Mr. PEARCE. Okay. But say there is not a crime. Say you have a suspicion that they are making methamphetamine out there in the middle of nowhere. Can you just go out?

Sheriff DANNELS. We do, yes.

Mr. PEARCE. Okay.

Sheriff DANNELS. It is part of Cochise County. I think every sheriff you ask would say the same thing, that if there is a crime within his county, in the middle of a military reservation, we go, we go.

Mr. PEARCE. Okay. But I am asking if you don't know there is a crime, can you go out there just to investigate?

Sheriff DANNELS. If we don't know there is a crime?

Mr. PEARCE. If you suspect, if you have somebody coming north out of the area and you suspect that there is probably something out there that needs to be looked at, do you just go on out there, or do you have to clear it with an agency?

Sheriff DANNELS. We go out there.

Mr. PEARCE. Okay. That is a different story than I hear most of the time.

Sheriff DANNELS. Yes, we do. This is where it is important where the locals, working with their Federal partners and their Federal leaders within the county boundaries, we all know each other very well and there is enough respect that we just go. We work close with them. If we need to get them involved, we will. But we don't let that stop us, is my point to this whole conversation.

Mr. PEARCE. Okay.

Mr. Del Cueto, just an observation. I am working my way through the list, so I am bouncing around a little bit here. But I was in the hearing when the Department of Homeland Security Secretary Napolitano testified in Congress, and we had probably 8 border sheriffs disputing her testimony, and she simply said they are lying. I mean, that was really, really, really not a good position for her to establish because I keep hearing the truth out here, and I am hearing the truth from here. But that is what makes it very difficult in Washington, that people get to a certain level and they have the established things that they are going to say regardless of what the truth is.

Sheriff Sam Yago, I remember him. He was probably 90 at that point. He was there to testify he was in law enforcement for 50 years and was dramatic, dramatic to hear that exchange where she just said you can't trust him. It was not good.

Would drones help you out when you are going up the side of the hill and they are going down the other side? The drone could be sitting up here so you would have somebody waiting on the other side and could see where they are going? I mean, that is what we are doing in Afghanistan, right?

Mr. DEL CUETO. Right. The bottom line, though, is we could have the drones up there, we could have drones in certain areas, but it is getting the manpower to go out there and arrest these individuals that the drones are seeing. That seems to be a big problem.

Mr. PEARCE. Okay.

Mr. DEL CUETO. Like I said earlier, a lot of our agents are farmed out.

Mr. PEARCE. So those farm-outs, we discussed that a minute ago. We went from 10,000, 12,000, up to 23,000 more or less. Are those productive farm-outs, or would they be better off brought back and put on the border, like I would recommend? But it might not be a good idea. What is your internal view?

Mr. DEL CUETO. On that, you would have to speak to the agencies, speak to the other agencies and the agencies we are farming them out to. So I know there are agents that are farmed out at the ports. There are some agents that are farmed out for DEA. There are agents that are farmed out at the prosecutor's office.

Mr. PEARCE. Right. So again, as I would visit with agents out in the field they said, okay, I spend about 3 hours a day on the border, the rest of the time is in paperwork. If I catch somebody, it takes me 6 or 7 hours to do the paperwork. Is that more or less accurate even if the numbers change pretty dramatically, that you catch them and you have to go in and do the paperwork?

Mr. DEL CUETO. It depends on the individuals we catch. On the average, you never know. It just depends on if they have priors. Obviously with some of these catch-and-release, you are not spending much time doing paperwork.

Mr. PEARCE. Because it seems like it takes a very special person to be there on the border, and then we put you on paperwork, which is not so special. I mean, I could do paperwork. I couldn't do your job, but I could do the paperwork. We take you with valuable, valuable capabilities and put you in doing what a clerk could do, frankly. I know you have to do some legal things, but——

Mr. DEL CUETO. Right.

Mr. PEARCE. So is that a possibility that we could redirect?

Mr. DEL CUETO. That is one of the reasons I spoke about the FOBs. I know a lot of money has been spent on these FOBs. They are in remote areas. Many times when these agents apprehend individuals in these remote areas, it would be easily accessible to go to these FOBs and do the processing from the FOB and do all the paperwork there. That way you are still close to the border and are able to move around. I think that would be a huge asset.

Mr. PEARCE. Do you ever have the top managers in the department come down and ask you if you all had to solve the problems of assets and how to secure the border? Do you ever have the Secretary of Homeland Security come down here and ask you all sitting right there?

Mr. DEL CUETO. Commissioner Kerlikowske was here last week and it was the first time I had ever seen him in the Tucson sector since he has been in that position.

Mr. PEARCE. Does he ask you what it would take? I mean, if I was there, I guarantee you, if I was running a business that required securing the border, I would be out here talking to people every day and making adjustments and putting the linebackers in or whatever the Chairwoman said.

Mr. DEL CUETO. Honestly, he spoke and he answered 3 questions, and that was it.

Mr. PEARCE. That is again what I find. The system is broken from Congress all the way across. Every system in Washington is absolutely broken because they don't ask the people who are there.

I want to wrap up with 1 additional question. Mayor, I have 2 questions actually. I am thinking about spending a little bit of money before I fly back to Washington this evening, and I may run out and get a haircut, so I need to know who you get your haircuts from.

[Laughter.]

Mr. PEARCE. I will do that in Douglas.

Mr. ORTEGA. My wife gives me mine.

Mr. PEARCE. Oh, then I guess I won't do that.

[Laughter.]

Mr. PEARCE. I will go to the airport and get a shoe shine instead.

[Laughter.]

Mr. PEARCE. So you hear the push. I know that business is a big deal, and I am a business guy, and I really respect that and appreciate that, and I appreciate your voice here today. Do you find that you are a little bit alarmed by the testimony coming around you that their testimony might influence people that they want to secure the border too much and they begin to interrupt the economic activity, or do you see that all can be done, we can have those wide-open gates and still secure the border? Is that a thing that you get alarmed about? Do you see where I am coming from? Because if they dominate the discussions and yours is left off on the side, then we begin to squeeze down business for security. So tell me a little bit about where you are there, and that will be the last question I have, Madam Chair.

Mr. ORTEGA. Yes. Actually, I am concerned with this, because I think a lot of times, especially election years, the border is painted in a very negative tone. There are a lot of good things that happen within our own communities culturally, with sports, with so many events, with the goods that are crossing on a daily basis that support our economy locally but also the economy of the United States of America. We are Americans. I think this is payback a bit for protecting the Phoenixes, the Tucsons, but there are a lot of us that live at the border, have lived there for generations, and sometimes I don't think we feel quite like Americans because we are kind-of-like ignored in many cases and we will deal with the problem behind us, but what about on the front line?

But we worry about commerce. We worry about people coming to visit. We are losing population in Cochise County, and we encourage people to come visit. Congressman McSally has been to Douglas many times. I don't think she has ever had any issues. We have gone out to many fine Mexican restaurants and never worry about things.

But I do understand the issues of the outlying areas as well.

Mr. PEARCE. Yes, you don't disregard them.

Mr. ORTEGA. No, not at all.

Mr. PEARCE. It is just that you want an equal seat at the table saying, fine, let's solve the problem, but also remember that commerce has got to occur.

Mr. ORTEGA. Yes, sir. That is why I appreciate being invited here today, so you hear the other side of the story. Thank you.

Mr. PEARCE. I grew up in 4–H and made my way through college showing pigs, and all I have to say is if you move 1,500 cows a day across that border, you are doing something right. So keep moving those cows.

Mr. ORTEGA. Thank you.

Ms. MCSALLY. Thanks. As a follow-up, that is why you are here, why all of you are here, and I appreciate it.

One last quick question, Mr. Del Cueto, before we go to the second panel. I just want to give you the opportunity. You mentioned agents moving into places in order to protect ranchers. Can you just give your perspective on the relationship between the Border Patrol Agents and ranchers right now, anything that could improve those relationships and the communication?

Mr. DEL CUETO. Well, you know, I work on the Tohono O'odham Reservation, so I work with some of the ranchers down there. But like I said, a lot of my constituents work in that area and throughout Cochise County, and it is really not banging heads with the ranchers. The agents are out there doing their jobs——

Ms. MCSALLY. It is not, or it is?

Mr. DEL CUETO. It is not a banging their heads is what I am getting from the agents. But there are certain areas that are closed off to Border Patrol Agents. That is the message that is being sent to them, that they can't work certain areas. So if you track a group near the border into these individuals' lands, you can't go in their land. So what you have to do is you have to drive around the entire area of their land and try to intercept them on the northern part. By the time you get there, a lot of these individuals are already gone, and that is a serious problem.

Another thing is if we encounter some of these individuals and we go on their land because we are actively following this group, and God forbid something would happen on this land where we would need air support or we would need medical attention, not just for ourselves but also to the individuals we would apprehend, it would be very limited and it would be very difficult to get the emergency vehicles on this land to assist any kind of injured individual.

Ms. MCSALLY. Great. Thank you.

Okay, we are done with Panel 1. Thanks for everybody's patience. I want to thank the witnesses for your testimony today and for the good discussion and questions. There may be some follow-up questions, I don't know. If you think of some, per procedures, they will submit them in writing, and then we will ask you guys to respond in writing if we have those.

So, with that, I will dismiss the first panel. Thanks for your testimony and your time.

I request that the Clerk prepare the witness table for our second panel, and then we will start again.

[Recess.]

Ms. MCSALLY. All right, we are going to get started again. I am pleased to welcome 5 distinguished witnesses for our second panel at today's hearing.

First, Mr. Dan Bell. He is the president of ZZ Cattle Corporation in Nogales, Arizona. Mr. Bell and his family work on his ranch. The ranch has been in his family since 1938, and they share a 10-

mile boundary line with the U.S.-Mexico border. He has also served as the president of the Southern Arizona Cattleman's Protective Association and is currently serving as past president of the Arizona Cattle Growers Association.

Mr. Mark Adams is the coordinator of Frontera De Cristo, a Presbyterian border ministry located in the sister cities of Agua Prieta, Sonora, and Douglas, Arizona. Mr. Adams is a native of—I should be calling you Pastor Adams, shouldn't I?—of Clover, South Carolina, and a graduate of Columbia Theological Seminary in Decatur, Georgia. He was ordained in 1998 and has served as the U.S. coordinator of Frontera De Cristo since that time.

Mr. Jaime Chamberlain is the president of Nogales, Arizona-based J–C Distributing, Inc., an importer of Mexican fruits and vegetables. Jaime is the past-chairman of the board of directors of the Fresh Produce Association of America and is a sponsor member of the Nogales Santa Cruz County Port Authority. He was recently appointed by Governor Ducey to the Arizona Rural Economic Development Advisory Council and the board of directors of the Arizona Mexico Commission, where he serves as co-chairman of the Ports and Transportation Infrastructure Committee.

Mrs. Nan Stockholm-Walden serves as the vice president and counsel at Farmers Investment Company, the largest pecan growing and processing farm in the world, located in Sahuarita, Arizona. During her career Nan served as counsel to the U.S. Senate Environment and Public Works Committee and Counsel for Senator Dan Patrick Moynihan on the Water Resources Subcommittee. She was chief of staff for Senator Bill Bradley, who served on the Senate Finance and Energy and Natural Resources Committees. She has also been an associate vice president for Federal relations at the University of Arizona in Tucson.

Mr. Frank Krentz is the son of Rob Krentz, who was tragically gunned down as he was trying to help an immigrant in 2010. Mr. Krentz has been working on the family ranch in Cochise County since his graduation from New Mexico State University. He is involved with the Apache School Board, the Borderlands Group, Arizona Cattle Growers, Brightwater Water Conservation District, and the vice president of the Arizona Association of Conservation Districts.

The Chair now recognizes Mr. Bell.

STATEMENT OF DANIEL G. BELL, PRESIDENT, ZZ CATTLE CORPORATION

Mr. BELL. Good morning, Chairwoman McSally, Congressman Pearce. Thank you for coming down and thank you for holding this subcommittee hearing. It is an issue that is very important to ranchers who live along the border or even near the border.

Again, my name is Daniel Bell. I am a third-generation rancher from Nogales, Arizona. Our family has been ranching the same piece of country since the late 1930s. We are located just west of the city of Nogales, and we have 10 miles of border that we share with Mexico. Of that, 2 miles of that border has a bollard-style fence or what you call a border wall. The remaining 8 miles is a 4-strand barbed-wire cattle fence.

Our ranch is subject to the impacts of illegal immigration and drug smuggling on a daily basis. In the 1990s, border operations in California and Texas essentially forced the illegal border traffic into Arizona. As a result, Arizona border cities were fortified, forcing the illegal activity onto the adjacent ranches, and we began seeing the UDA groups increase from groups of 1 or 2 to groups of 50 or more at that time.

As a result of these increases, the ranches were heavily impacted. We have damage being done to our fences. Our watering facilities were damaged and drained very often. Vehicles are stolen, homes are broken into, and valuables are taken. Also since then, the frequency of fire has increased on the ranches along the border as a result of warming fires that have been let go, fires lit by UDAs in distress, and fires lit by drug smugglers to create a distraction or diversion.

We have had a house burned to the ground, and in 2011 approximately two-thirds of our ranch was burned from 13 different fires that year. In fact, just this past Tuesday there was a fire started by illegals on the western portion of our ranch. Border Patrol was able to apprehend the individuals and called in the fire. The Forest Service was able to get on it rapidly and get it put out.

Violence in the border region was also on an increase. In 1998, while apprehending drug smugglers, Border Patrol Agent Alexander Kirpnick was murdered in one of our grazing pastures. A decade later border agents were taking fire, and some agents were even wounded in sniper-style shootings near the border. In March 2010, my friend Rob Krentz was murdered on his ranch in Cochise County doing what Frank and I still do to this day, checking our pastures and checking our cattle.

One month later, the foreman of the ranch neighboring us in Mexico was found murdered and buried in a shallow grave, and he had been missing for over a month. Later that year, Border Patrol Agent Brian Terry was murdered on our neighbor's ranch just to the north of us while he and his team were working to rid the area of violent rip crews that were targeting illegal aliens and drug smugglers.

The facts I have just stated were the breaking points that caused ranchers along the border to demand more border security resources and more boots on the ground. It has been my experience that improvement can happen with better access and by establishing roads along the international boundary with Mexico. Being able to get to the border is paramount if one expects to defend it. With better access, a good border road system in place, and next-generation technologies like a remote video surveillance system and towers that are capable of detecting movement within their field of view, as well as radar equipment, mobile surveillance-capable vehicles, as well as integrated fixed towers that could be put into place, this technology can detect movement and focus in on that movement to maximize efficiency by verifying if a response is necessary and, if so, providing the critical situational awareness needed.

Better access and roads along the border would place law enforcement efforts closer to the line of scrimmage and reduce the footprint of the illegal activity, which is a positive for the environment. Where access is limited and roads are non-existent, it is extremely important that air assets like helicopters are available to insert agents into rugged and remote areas and provide support for agents on the ground. Fixed-wing aircraft and drones must also be readily available to detect and respond to illegal activity and direct law enforcement to intercept points and provide a much-needed situational awareness.

Of course, having more boots on the ground in the right place at the right time in order to intercept the illegal activity is critical.

Some of the other measures include increasing horse patrols in the rugged and remote areas where access is limited; the use of military personnel in the border security mission; establish better communications and technology not only for law enforcement but for the civilians that are out there as well; and establish more forward operating bases to cut travel and response times to incidents.

Fund State and Federal attorney offices to ensure timely prosecution of border-related offenses, and ensure that the judicial resources are in place to provide consequences to offenders.

We need to figure out a set of metrics that will maintain resource levels even after we see improvement, because what tends to happen is that when you get improvement, we tend to pull resources away, and then we are stuck with the same problem.

One of the things that has worked very well for us in the Nogales area is the citizen advisory boards and the ranch liaison programs, and I also see that as a valuable metric because we can see what is happening and we can relay that information to law enforcement.

Over time I have witnessed improvement in certain areas, and it has coincided with the implementation of some of the measures that I mentioned to you today. It is only on a small portion of our ranch, but we need to keep working and keep bringing those measures into place.

I thank you for allowing me the time to come and address you today. Thank you.

[The prepared statement of Mr. Bell follows:]

PREPARED STATEMENT OF DANIEL G. BELL

MAY 9, 2016

Good morning my name is Daniel Bell. I am a third-generation rancher from Nogales Arizona and president of the ZZ Cattle Corporation. Our family has been ranching on the same piece of country since the late 1930s, just west of the city of Nogales along the border with Mexico. Our ranch has approximately 10 miles of actual border with Mexico and with the exception of a 2-mile stretch of bollard fence and a few hundred yards of vehicle barrier, the remainder of the international boundary with Mexico is comprised of a 4-strand barb-wire cattle fence. Our ranch consists primarily of Federal grazing permits with the USDA Forest Service, private lands, and State trust land all of which are subject to impacts revolving around illegal immigration and drug smuggling.

As far back as we can remember we have always had impacts with regard to illegal immigration and drug smuggling. However, in the 1990s things changed drastically! The implementation of Operation Gatekeeper in California and Operation Hold the Line in Texas essentially forced illegal border traffic into Arizona. As a result of increased illegal border traffic, fortified fencing of cities along border began to occur, forcing the illegal activity on to the adjacent ranch lands. In areas where it was common to see 1 or 2 undocumented aliens, were now seeing groups sometimes ranging in the number of 50 or more. With those increases in numbers, also came increases in property damage, theft, fire frequency, and violence. Our fences were being cut, watering facilities were being tampered with and drained, our houses were being broken into and valuables were taken, we even had vehicles stolen. On one occasion the wife of one of our employees was forced at knife point to prepare meals for a few individuals. Upon arriving home our employee tracked the group and lead authorities to their location.

Over the years violence in the border region had been on the increase. Nogales Station agents had been fired upon and in a few incidents agents were wounded by apparent sniper-style shootings. In 1998, Border Patrol Agent Alexander Kirpnick was murdered as he was apprehending drug smugglers in one of our grazing pastures. On March 27, 2010 while checking livestock, watering facilities, and fences, my friend Rob Krentz was murdered on his ranch in Cochise County. On May 12, 2010, the ranch foreman from one of the ranches in Mexico that neighbors us along the border was found murdered and buried in a shallow grave after he had gone missing a month earlier. On December 17, 2010, Border Patrol Agent Brian Terry, a member BORTAC, the elite tactical unit of the Border Patrol, was murdered on the ranch that neighbors us to the North. His team was in the area to rid the area of violent rip-off crews that were targeting undocumented aliens and drug carriers.

Also, over the years the fire frequency has increased on the ranches along the border as a result of warming fires not being extinguished, fires lit by undocumented aliens in distress, and fires lit by smugglers to create diversions. In the mid-2000's, an unoccupied house on the Bear Valley portion of our ranch was set ablaze by undocumented aliens when they attempted to light the propane powered lights. In 2011, we witnessed one of the worst fire seasons ever. I believe there were 13 different fires that year that burned approximately two-thirds of the entire ranch. Only one of those fires was considered to be a naturally caused fire, all the others were either diversion fires or distress fires. In fact just this past Tuesday, May 3, 2016 there was a fire started on the western portion of the ranch, by illegal aliens. Border Patrol was able to apprehend them and report the fire to the Forest Service who responded quickly and contained the fire to about 30 acres.

The issues I have touched on have caused ranchers along the border to be very vocal about increasing border security resources and placing more boots on the ground.

My main focus here today is to highlight what I consider to be useful and positive measures to help secure the border and the lands we work on. Measures like creating access and establishing roads along the international boundary with Mexico. Being able to get to the border is paramount if one expects to defend it. The areas of the border that are more secure are the areas that were less difficult to secure. What remains is probably some of the most rugged terrain encountered along the border, most of which is inaccessible by vehicles. Not only is it rugged, but much of it is Federal land, which brings with it other obstacles and restrictions for border security. Delays due to lengthy Environmental Impact Studies, operational restrictions due to Wilderness Designations and concerns for so-called threatened and endangered species all stand in the way securing the border.

Access and infrastructure in the form of roads is drastically needed along the border, otherwise the area of operation remains unwieldy. Roads also allow for faster response times when a threat approaches the border. With a good road system in place, implementation of technology in the form of Remote Video Surveillance Systems, Integrated Fixed Towers, and Mobile Surveillance Capable Vehicles can be facilitated. In order to secure the border, law enforcement must be nimble as to address shifts in patterns of illegal activity and also have situational awareness. Again the reality of gaining access and constructing infrastructure along the border on Federal lands is a lengthy process and it needs to be streamlined.

For over a decade I have witnessed the implementation these measures, including the construction of 2 miles of a bollard fence. The Coronado National Forest, Nogales Ranger Station, and the Border Patrol are to be commended for these accomplishments. I can attest to the effectiveness of these measures and how illegal traffic has been reduced in these areas and has given law enforcement more focus along that portion of the border. That focus reduces the footprint of the illegal activity as well as the footprint required for law enforcement which is a positive for the environment. More of the Federal and State land management agencies need to adopt this strategy.

Unfortunately, some of the traffic shifted to the areas that are more remote and rugged where these measures do not exist. Until access and roads can be implemented in these areas, it is extremely important that air assets like helicopters, and fixed-wing air craft, as well as, drones are available to detect illegal activity, direct law enforcement to intercept points, provide the much-needed situatonal awareness, and even insert agents into these problem areas.

In the past military personnel were used in the remote areas as Entry Identification Teams with the purpose of calling out illegal activity, allowing agents to respond directly and again providing agents with that situational awareness. In fact, many if not most of the Remote Video Surveillance System Towers were constructed on the very sites that were previously occupied by the entry identification teams.

As these areas are remote and rugged, they often lack the necessary communications technology for both law enforcement and civilians. This is important as there are citizens out recreating in the forest despite the travel caution signage warnings of smuggling and illegal immigration in the area.

Of course the most important factor is having boots on the ground, in the right place, at the right time in order to intercept the illegal activity. Border Patrol must increase horse patrols in the rugged and remote areas where access is limited. Also, Forward Operating Bases have been used in the past and were effective, cutting response times and travel times to areas of deployment by several hours.

There is a need to maintain the morale of the men and women working to secure the border. Funding State and Federal Attorneys' Offices must be adequate to assure timely prosecution of border-related offenses. As part of that, ensuring that there are judicial resources in place to provide consequences to offenders is imperative.

It is also important to ensure that metrics are in place that account for the reductions in illegal activity and maintain resources as border conditions improve. I am fortunate to be a part of the Citizens Advisory Boards and the Rancher Liaison Group for the Nogales Border Patrol Station. It gives me the opportunity to address security issues in areas of our operation and allows Border Patrol the ability to communicate with the public and the folks most effected by illegal activity. I view these groups as another sort of metric.

As I have stated before. I have witnessed improvement over the past few years in certain areas and it has coincided with the implementation of the measures that I have mentioned to you here today.

Thank you for your time and allowing me to come before you today!

Ms. MCSALLY. Thanks, Mr. Bell.

The Chair now recognizes Pastor Adams.

STATEMENT OF MARK STEPHEN ADAMS, COORDINATOR, FRONTERA DE CRISTO

Mr. ADAMS. Thank you, Chair McSally and Representative Pearce, for the opportunity to be here. As I push the button, I see that I am talking with a Shure microphone. Twenty-some years ago my wife, Miriam Maldonado Escobar, migrated from Chiapas, Mexico after her family could no longer farm on corn farms there because of the price of corn dropping and came to the border to work for Shure. They had a factory on the U.S.-Mexico border in Agua Prieta Sonora. Shure was part of the reason that I got the love of my life.

For me, I have been living on the border of the United States and Mexico for 18 years. For the first 18 years of my life, I lived on the border between South Carolina and North Carolina, quite different borders. But also, the border between the United States and Mexico is also quite different now than it was 20 years ago, 25 years ago, 30 years ago. It is very different. It has changed dramatically.

What is the border for me? The border is home. The border is a place that I love. The border is a place where 12 million other folks live and, I imagine, love as well. So the border is home. So as you all undertake the task of making walls and trying to oversee the policies that make our border secure, I really want to encourage you to always remember that the border is home. It is home to me and it is home to millions of others. Too often, the border has been seen as a place to defend, to be afraid of, as opposed to a place to revitalize, a place to see as an asset, a place of encounter. For me, that is what the border is.

Unfortunately, I am afraid that at times our attempts to secure the border for whatever fear we might have has negatively impacted the local communities on the border. As Mr. Pearce saw with Mayor Danny Ortega, the town of Douglas is secure in the sense of crossings and crime, but also at times for us to have a secure border we also have to have the secure and safe and efficient flow of people through our borders. For many, many years we have neglected that part.

So as we have secured our border between ports of entry, or tried to, we have neglected securing our communities' security and our economic security. So I want to encourage you to think about the importance of that aspect of border security as you go about your task there.

Also, as you seek to do your task to secure our border, please do not sacrifice the civil rights of our home, of our community, of our people. I was serving with a group of folks who came down from the Border Action Network. They wanted to meet some of the folks from the community in Douglas to see what it was their relationship was with increased enforcement in our community and if there were any problems. So I said, sure, I will go around the community with you. As we were going, someone asked me, well, Mark, have you had any problems with your local Border Patrol? No. I said we meet on a regular basis; they are very helpful.

You have never had any problems, he said? I said, well, there was that time where I was driving the Frontera de Cristo van and got stopped 3 times within 45 minutes. That was a little strange. Then there was the time where I picked up a friend of mine from the Philippines at the shuttle and I got followed back to our office and the car sat in front of our office. When I went out and said excuse me but can I help you, they said we heard that there is a smuggling ring going on here, and I said no, that is all right. That was kind of strange.

Then there was the time—and I went off and rattled off 5 times where I experienced something very different than I would ever have experienced in South Carolina or North Carolina. I say that as a white man who has 20 years of education, formal education, who is a U.S. citizen, who speaks English, who has a national church at his back. The reality is many of our community who don't have those same privileges that I have—there is no reason I should have them and others not—face realities that are dangerous for our community security, and we need to improve our relationship with our local law enforcement.

Finally, I want to say that we need to take death out of the immigration equation. Too many people have died in our deserts because we have used deserts and mountains as a lethal deterrent. They have been lethal but not deterrents, and that doesn't uphold who we are as a Nation. We need to always remember that you have the challenge of securing our borders but also upholding the legacy of us as a Nation of immigrants.

So I want to please ask you to think about the security of the tired, the poor, the huddled masses yearning to breathe free, take them out of the drug equation, take them out and allow for a safe and efficient flow of people through ports of entry to decrease the suffering and the death that occurs because of policies that are harming folks who can no longer make a living or are trying to be reunited with family.

Thank you for your time.

[The prepared statement of Mr. Adams follows:]

PREPARED STATEMENT OF MARK STEPHEN ADAMS

MAY 9, 2016

INTRODUCTION

Chair McSally and Members of the committee, I am Mark Adams, a Presbyterian pastor serving with the bi-national ministry Frontera de Cristo, based in Douglas, AZ/Agua Prieta, Sonora. I lived the first 18 years of my life on the South Carolina/North Carolina border and for the past 18 years I have lived on the U.S./Mexico border in Douglas, AZ/Agua Prieta, Sonora. While I crossed the South Carolina/North Carolina border at frequently growing up, I cross the U.S./Mexico border almost daily and sometimes up to 4 times a day. I am grateful for the opportunity to address the committee about life on the border.

In 1998, I migrated to the Douglas/Agua Prieta to serve with the church. I did not realize before coming that political and economic forces had converted our towns and surrounding areas into the primary crossing point for persons entering the United States without proper documentation.

The church of the U.S./Mexico borderlands has been in a unique position to witness to the growing division, fear, and death occurring on our shared border as well as in the interiors of our nations. It is in this context of tension and suffering that I and all those who are Christian are called to bear witness to the good news of Jesus Christ who "is our peace who has made the two one and who has broken down the dividing wall of hostility." (Ephesians 2:14).

Being part of the church that crosses national, political, social, linguistic, and cultural borders has enabled us to experience the suffering on both sides of the border—whether it is crying with family members in Mexico who have lost loved ones in the deserts or listening to the frustration of property owners in the United States who have lost a sense of physical and financial security because of persons crossing through their property; whether celebrating in worship with migrants who give witness to how God saved their lives again or praying with Border Patrol Agents who sometimes fear for their safety; or grieving with families on both sides of the border as they struggle with the violence of an underground drug culture. Because we are in relationship with people on multiple sides of the "issues" and have become familiar with the realities and complexity of the situation, it has become impossible for us to scapegoat any group of people.

As Christians we are called to work together across national boundaries and to address our common concerns as sisters and brothers equally created in the Divine image. We are not adversaries. Furthermore, we are called to resist the temptation to demonize or dehumanize any individual or group of individuals. By building relationships and understanding across borders, those most affected by the brokenness of current policies can unite to struggle for change that is beneficial to people on both sides of the border.

THE IMPORTANCE OF REMEMBERING OUR HISTORY

Each year we host around 500 people from churches, seminaries, universities, schools, and leadership organizations as part of our mission education ministry. Over the last year, we have hosted:

young and old;

progressive, liberal, conservative, libertarian, and a mixture of political philosophies;

Presbyterian, Jewish, Muslim, Catholic, Agonostic, Atheist, Mennonite, Episcopalian;

Methodist, Inquiring, and Skeptical.

One of our main goals in our ministry in general and specifically in our mission education ministry is to build relationships and understanding across borders. As part of our orientation, we go to a spot just north of the U.S./Mexico border and stand in the shadow of the tall multi-million dollar rusted steel fence that we as a Government built in 2012 as part of the border infrastructure after the original "aesthetic" fence initially erected in 1997 was torn down.

While standing there, we ask folks to share a part of who they are: Their names, where they were born, where they live now, and where their ancestors came from before they came to what is now the United States of America and why their ancestors came. It is an exercise of rememberence . . . remembering our own immigrant stories, because we are a people who so easily forget.

It hardly ever ceases to amaze me the diversity that emerges. As we remember our origins: Ireland, Italy, the West Coast of Africa, China, Germany, Poland, Japan, I simultaneously rejoice in the reality that we are a nation of immigrants with the Statue of Liberty as one of our enduring symbols and remember that many of our ancestors were welcomed not with the sentiment of the Emma Lazurus poem "give me the tired, the poor, the huddled masses yearning to breathe free . . . " that forms one of the highest ideals of our who we are as a Nation, but rather with the crass xenophobia that also has strong currents within our National identity.

Roy Goodman is a colleague on the border shocked me one day with a t-shirt he was wearing. On the t-shirt it had two proud symbols of our country: The U.S. flag and the Statue of Liberty. Underneath these symbols: There was a quote that said:

"'Few of their Children in the Country learn English . . . The Signs in our Streets have Inscriptions in both Languages, and in some places only [their language] . . . In short, unless the Stream of their Importation could be turned . . . they will soon so outnumber us, that all the advantages we have, will not in my Opinion be able to preserve our Language, and even our Government will become precarious."[1]

"Roy, how could you wear that horrible t-shirt?" I asked in disbelief, feeling as if he was betraying our work of building bridges between peoples.

"You know who said that?" he responded. "Benjamin Franklin. He was talking about the Germans in Pennsylvania."

The 15% of the U.S. population that can trace part of its lineage back to Germany[2] is probably very glad that neither the Native Americans, nor the colonies nor the young U.S. Government later had a quota in the eighteenth century of deporting 400,000 people a year that some of our founders and I imagine many of the populace thought did not belong in our Nation. In hindsight it is easy to see the misguided nature of the parts of our history that include the oppression, exclusion, and/or fear of immigrant peoples because of their racial, ethnic, cultural, or national origin: Whether forced immigrants brought to our shores as slaves, or the Irish who "needed not to apply" (ironically I have often heard the vehicles used by our Border Patrol to Transport people who have been apprehended as Paddy Wagons), or the Chinese who were the first group of people legally targeted by the Chinese Exclusion Act of 1882, but the cliché often is true: History repeats itself.

As you seek to fulfill your responsibilities as members of the Border and Maritime Security Subcommittee, I urge you, to remember, remember not to be guided by the basest of our nature which often fears the other, remember that we are a Nation of immigrants, that when we are at our best we believe that "all men [and women] are created equal", and that E Pluribus Unum. I urge you to help us on the border and throughout the Nation to secure a legacy of truly being a Nation of immigrants that respects the human rights of all; help us to live into the reality that we can be a city on a hill.

MEANING OF BORDERS

What Do Borders Mean to You?

While still standing in the shadow of the twenty-foot tall multi-million dollar rusted fence that has come to define much of our border with Mexico, I ask our visiting delegations: "What do borders mean to you?"

I intentionally make borders plural, because borders exist in their own communities: The border between property, or neighborhoods, or town and county or States. However, standing in the shadow of what Pete Vogel, an immigrant from Germany and good friend of Frontera de Cristo, calls our "Berlin Wall", people's responses are almost always focused on the meaning of the U.S./Mexico border. Some common themes are: A division of hostility; a separation of us from them; an effort of the rich to keep from the poor.

---

[1] Excerpt from a letter to Peter Collinson from Benjamin Franklin written May 9, 1753.
[2] According to U.S. Census Data *http://factfinder.census.gov/faces/tableservices/jsf/pages/productview.xhtml?pid=DEC_00_SF3_PCT018&prodType=table.*

One of our visitors said: "There is something that I really don't like about the wall . . . but what if it did not exist, wouldn't everyone just come to the United States?"

For some it is hard to remember that for almost 150 years between the signing of the Treaty of Guadalupe and the beginning of the massive border infrastructure build-up during the Clinton administration in the mid-1990's, there was no multi-million-dollar taxpayer-funded steel fence between us and our neighbors to the south, nor was there massive camera surveillance, nor drones, nor miles of multi-million dollar high-speed all-purpose roads paralleling the border, nor the over 21,000 Border Patrol Agents that we have today.[3] It is amazing for me to hear some politicians speak today as if we as a Nation have done nothing to "secure our border".

I am often invited to speak in different venues in the interior of the United States and almost always ask people what they think of when they think of the border. Much like the majority of the visitors with us, the border has negative connotations for most of the people on the interior with whom I talk. I have people who question why I would ever choose to live on the border and others who ask if I am afraid.

The meaning and implications of borders change and mean different things to different people. The political, cultural, demographic, and economic context of our Nation always determines the meaning and implications of our borders. The border between the United States and Mexico has a very different meaning with starkly different implications in 2016 than it did when its most recent demarcation was set by the Gadsden Purchase over 150 years ago.

When the border between the United States and Mexico was finalized in the 1850s, it was a political border that marked where the spheres of influence and power of the United States and Mexico began and ended, not the heavily-fortified border that divides communities and families today.

So what does the border mean to me?

It means home.

With all of its joys and suffering, its opportunities and challenges, the border is my home and it is home to over 12 million people along the U.S./Mexico border. I think that those who have made the laws and policies regarding border security have often forgotten that the border is home to millions of people. Too often the voice of a few border residents claiming that the border is "out of control" and needs to be secured is given more importance than the voices of the broad spectrum of our community who understand that cross-border economic, cultural, and social cooperation is our life-blood and the safe and efficient flow of people through our ports of entry is essential.

Our efforts at "border security" have often impeded our community security and have had a detrimental impact on the poor as well as people of color.

I urge you as you go about the tasks of your committee to please remember that the border is our home, it is not a place to be militarized, but rather a place to be revitalized.

INCREASED BORDER SECURITY AND ITS BROAD CONSEQUENCES

For 150 years there had been a pretty fluid border between United States and Mexico. For most of our history, crossing the U.S./Mexico border was not too unlike crossing the North Carolina/South Carolina border. Beginning in the 1990s, things changed dramatically for us on the border and the border began to be more robustly enforced through efforts like Operation Hold The Line, Operation Gatekeeper, and Operation Safeguard. Our change in border policy corresponded with economic forces that were pulling people north to the United States (low unemployment and demand for labor) and pushing people north from Mexico (dramatic loss of agricultural jobs). People were forced to cross through the desert areas of Agua Prieta/Douglas, Arizona in the late 1990s and early 2000s, but by the mid- and late-2000s the flow of migration was pushed to even more remote and deadly areas like the deserts and mountains east of Yuma and the Altar Valley southwest of Tucson.

With the signing of the Illegal Immigration Reform and Immigrant Responsibility Act of 1996, President Clinton began a massive increase in the budget for border protection. Under the Bush and Obama administrations, we have continued the policy of increasing the budget and the number of Border Patrol Agents.

Unlike the Immigration Reform and Control Act signed by President Reagan in 1986 that provided a pathway to legalization for persons who were in the United States without authorization prior to the Act, Clinton's "reform" provided no such

---

[3] According to CBP website *https://www.cbp.gov/border-security/along-us-borders/overview*.

relief and only focused on the removal of persons in the United States without authorization and the deterrence of future undocumented immigrants.

Has the strategy been effective? Despite our attempts to "secure" the border, the presence of undocumented immigrants in the United States is millions more now than it was when we began Operation Gatekeeper in 1994.

In 1994, I was teaching Spanish in my hometown of Clover, South Carolina just south of the North Carolina border. Other than myself and one other non-native Spanish-speaking teacher, there were no other Spanish-speaking persons in town. I went back there 10 years later, in 2004. Ten years after we started beefing up our border security programs and implementing Operation Gatekeeper, there was a large banner decorated with Mexican and Guatemalan flags hanging from the roof of the Piggly Wiggly grocery store, with the words: "Tenemos productos hispanos"—we have Hispanic products. The First Baptist church was offering free English as a Second Language classes. At the bank, a sign asked if you wanted service in English or Spanish. In 10 years, Clover, South Carolina had gone from having 2 non-native Spanish-speaking people to having a sizeable enough population that grocery stores and banks were marketing to them and churches were reaching out to them.

And this anecdote could be repeated in many towns, suburbs, and cities throughout the United States, precisely at a time when our Government decided to get serious about enforcing the border.

In 1994, there were 4.5 million undocumented persons in the United States. Now, after spending billions of dollars to "secure" the border, there are more than 11 million—the number had increased to over 12 million prior to the recession that began in 2008.

There has been other serious and even deadly consequences to our decision to pursue a border enforcement strategy that uses the deserts and mountains as lethal deterrents without considering the power of the economic and family push and pull factors.

Increased Death and Injury

Since the inception of Operation Gatekeeper in 1994, more than 3 times more people have died in the deserts of the southwest while seeking to reach the "American Dream" than the number of persons who died in the attacks of 9/11. More people have died crossing the U.S./Mexico border trying to provide a livelihood for their families than the combined number of U.S. soldiers who have died in the Iraq and Afghanistan wars. Since 1994, over 7,000 bodies have been found. That doesn't include the deaths of persons whose bodies have never been found.

Each Tuesday at 5:15 pm, a group gathers 5 blocks north of the border for the Healing Our Borders Vigil in which we remember the persons by name who have died in Cochise County while crossing, we pray for their families, we pray for an end to deaths in the desert, we pray for our Government and the government of Mexico and we recommit ourselves to work for healthier relationships among our peoples and countries.

Our policy of using the deserts and mountains as lethal deterrents and increasing height of fencing have also resulted in a significant increase in the number of persons sustaining traumatic physical injuries while crossing the border. In addition to the intense suffering experienced by the migrants who have not been deterred by our policies that intentionally increase the risk for their crossing, border hospitals have experienced financial and emotional stress as they receive more patients with broken bones or severe complications from hypothermia and hyperthermia. The increasing number of life-threatening and life-altering injuries also has a psychological impact on our agents who are tasked with securing our borders, as they are often the first responders to migrants with compound fractures, severe dehydration, and other painful physical conditions.

One of our ministries is the Migrant Resource Center, which is the first non-governmental building that you arrive to when you enter Agua Prieta by foot. In June we will celebrate our 10th Anniversary of providing a safe place for men, women, and children who have been returned to Mexico by our Border Patrol. In that time, we have welcomed over 86,000 men, women, and children. Together with our partners at the Kino Initiative in Nogales who have welcomed many more people and especially now that almost all repatriation is happening through Nogales we can testify about the physical and emotional trauma of our broken border and immigration system.

I met Guillerma in the Migrant Resource Center.

"Hey Marcos, she's from South Carolina!"

Adrian Gonzalez one of the volunteers pulled on my shoulder and announced excitedly the news that another one of my "paisanos" was less than 7 feet away from me. We were both in the Migrant Resource Center, yet we were miles apart in the reasons for finding ourselves in the center.

I turned and saw a woman not too much younger than me standing in dark clothes and a baseball cap shading a hint of deep sadness in her face. 60% of the skin on her hands had been scrapped off as she slid down the posts of our border fence.

"*Buenos dias! Me llamo Marcos, como se llama Ud.?*", I asked, assuming that this fellow Sandlapper's first language was Spanish.

"My name is Guillermina," she responded in perfect English. Guillermina, had moved to South Carolina about the time I moved to Agua Prieta. She had been living in Myrtle Beach for 10 years, working in a hotels and restaurants—the irony of her working in the hospitality industry is a painful reality. She loves living in South Carolina despite not always feeling welcome, she has had work to help feed her family—Jose, her husband, and Kevin, her 6-year-old son.

She had not seen her dad in more than 16 years and had crossed back to Mexico because her dad had had a heart attack. Tears welled up in her eyes and in the eyes of most of us gathered in that humbled building.

With her voice trembling, she said, "When I left, he said,
'Hija this will probably be the last time we see each other. Be a good mother to my grandson. I love you.'
My world is torn in two—my dad is on this side of the border and my son and husband are over on the other side."

Pastor Brandi Casto Waters of First PC Greer, SC, who was visiting us that day led us all in prayer with and for Guillermina and we joined together in the hope for the day when the border would be a place of encounter and peace and not a place of division and conflict.

As I left, I let Guillermina know that I had a son Kevin's age and that I would keep them in my prayers, I also let her know that I and the ministry with whom I serve are committed to continue the hard work of changing laws that tears worlds apart. I asked her if she would like me to share her story with you—"please ask them to pray for us."

On November 20, 2014, President Obama announced an Executive Order that will provide an opportunity for almost 4 million parents like Guillermina to come out of the shadows and not have to live in fear of being separated from their children. I know that most on the committee disagree with the policy and that it is being challenged in court. I also know that it is an imperfect solution, and Congress needs to act to align our laws more with the gospel's call to radical hospitality and with Emma Lazuras' words on one of the iconic symbols of our Nation: "give me your tired, your poor, your huddled masses yearning to breathe free."

Use of Force

In addition to the deaths and injury due to the increased physical challenges of crossing in more remote and perilous places, there has also been an increase of deaths and injury due to use of force. We urge you to advocate for the full implementation of the February 2013 PERF report and that this committee demand that CBP become more transparent and accountable and implement a complaint filing process that is accessible and effective.

Boon to the Smuggling Industry

An irony of our increased border enforcement is that it has been accompanied by an increase in the size, sophistication, and wealth of smuggling operations on both sides of the border. Smuggling of drugs and people is a growth industry. In its working paper "Analysis of Migrant Smuggling Costs Along the Southwest Border," the Department of Homeland Security[4] provides data tracking the increased costs of smuggling with the increase of border enforcement. The data presented in the DHS paper corresponds closely with the information of the local residents in Agua Prieta with whom I have talked over the years. According to them, the cost to get across the border has risen from $50 to $100 prior to 1994, if a smuggler was needed at all, to $800 in 1998 when I first arrived on the border, to $2,000 or more today—with a much higher risk of being caught, injured, or killed. The DHS's working paper states that the increased costs for smuggling are only a "potential deterrent."

Strained Relationships Between Federal Law Enforcement and Local Communities

I believe that it is essential for both community security and border security that there be a good relationship between the Federal law enforcement and local community—more than 85% of the population of Douglas is of Mexican descent and while

---

[4] *http://www.dhs.gov/xlibrary/assets/statistics/publications/ois-smuggling-wp.pdf.*

most are U.S. citizens there are families of mixed legal statuses. Racial profiling is a fear and lived experience for many of our community. Rosie Mendoza, a naturalized citizen originally from Mexico and a member of the board of Frontera de Cristo, shared in a community listening session with Chair McSally in February of 2015 about the experience of her U.S.-born sons, who have dark complexions being stopped dozens of times while walking on the street. She said their "crime" is "walking in Douglas while brown."

In a gathering we arranged for local Douglas business persons and the chief of staff of former Representative Barber, the business owners expressed concern about how they are treated as "guilty until proven innocent" when they are returning to the United States from Mexico. Their concern was not only for their persons, but also for business in Douglas in general. If they as business owners feel more apprehension coming back into the United States than going into Mexico, how must noncitizens feel and how many people might that feeling prevent from crossing the border to shop in the United States?

In my own family, we experience the tension of experiencing the reality of the border in very different ways. In a recent conversation with a church, my wife, Miriam, and I were asked us a seemingly simple question: "Is it easy for you to cross the border?" Miriam is a permanent resident of the United States and citizen of Mexico of indigenous descent.

We looked at each other knowingly and I asked her to answer the question. "It depends if it's him or me." Our children even experience a difference—our oldest daughter who is 20 has a dark complexion and our youngest 2 children have lighter complexions. Our oldest daughter has had experiences crossing the border in which she has been yelled at and humiliated, so much that I do not like her to cross the border (north) without me. I will not have the same concern for my 2 youngest children who are 12 and 8 when they become old enough to cross the border alone.

When we drive through the checkpoint outside of Tombstone, we make sure the I am driving and not my wife—and not because I am a better driver. Almost always when I am driving, we get waved through the checkpoint with "have a good day". When Miriam is driving we almost always get asked citizenship status. Febe, my sister-in-law who has driven through the checkpoint alone, was amazed to see how easy it was when I was driving. "That's white privilege" she chimed in from the back seat.

I was recently in a new local restaurant in Douglas when I heard a Border Patrol Agent comment to the waitress that he was glad that there was a new restaurant in Douglas. The waitress asked the agent: "How many restaurants can Border Patrol Agents eat at in Douglas?" While I had known about the reality that Border Patrol Agents did not feel welcome at many of restaurants and had unofficially but actively boycotted a couple, I was surprised to her the Agent's response: "Three."

I think it is incumbent upon us (both we as local residents and our Federal law enforcement) to work on strengthening our relationship and growing trust among us. I am proud to have worked with Mayor Ortega, the Douglas City Council and other organizations to have a resolution passed to make Douglas "A Welcoming Community". Initially it was in response to the negative impacts that Arizona's law SB1070 had on relationships with our neighbors to the south. We wanted them to know that Douglas welcomed them. However, as we continued our conversations we realized that we needed to expand our understand of welcome to include the Federal law enforcement in our midst.

Currently less than 25% of Federal agents stationed in Douglas live in Douglas. Most live in the Sierra Vista area. There are many reasons: Lack of housing attractive for agents; of jobs for spouses; of shopping options etc. I believe we both as a local community and as the Federal Government look for ways to make living in the communities where our agents work a more chosen option. By increasing the percentage of agents living locally, we are more likely to increase our understanding of and trust for one another. When we participate in civic groups together, when our children go to school together or play on the soccer team or take swim lessons, when we worship together, when we celebrate the fourth of July or Douglas Days together, when we get to know one another, it becomes harder to treat one another as enemies.

COMPREHENSIVE IMMIGRATION REFORM IS ESSENTIAL TO BORDER SECURITY

Many politicians have argued that there can be no immigration reform until the border is secure. This is a false dichotomy. Comprehensive immigration reform is actually integral to helping make the border more secure.

The Presbyterian Church has joined the majority of faith traditions advocating for comprehensive immigration reform. The basic elements of the resolution passed at our 216th General Assembly[5] are:

a. an opportunity for hard-working immigrants who are already contributing to this country to come out of the shadows, regularize their status upon satisfaction of reasonable criteria, and, over time, pursue an option to become lawful permanent residents and eventually United States citizens;

b. reforms in our family-based immigration system to significantly reduce waiting times for separated families who currently wait many years to be reunited;

c. the creation of legal avenues for workers and their families who wish to migrate to the United States to enter our country and work in a safe, legal, and orderly manner with their rights fully protected; and

d. border protection policies that are consistent with humanitarian values and with the need to treat all individuals with respect, while allowing the authorities to carry out the critical task of identifying and preventing entry of terrorists and dangerous criminals, as well as pursuing the legitimate task of implementing American immigration policy.

e. a call for living wages and safe working conditions for workers of United States-owned companies in other countries;

f. a call for greater economic development in poor countries to decrease the economic desperation, which forces the division of families and migration.

Most of the Border Patrol Agents that I have talked to have struggled emotionally with the part of their job that requires them to apprehend men and women who are migrating for economic reasons or to be reunited with family. The persons that they really want to apprehend are the people who are coming into the country with ill intent, smuggling drugs, or with criminal backgrounds.

By creating a system that would allow for the orderly, safe, and efficient flow of persons who are migrating for economic or family reasons through ports of entry and removing them from between ports of entry, we will not only reduce the emotional stress for many of our agents which will increase their job satisfaction and their effectiveness, but also enable them to focus on the real threats to our security.

Ms. McSALLY. Thanks, Pastor Adams.

The Chair now recognizes Mr. Chamberlain.

STATEMENT OF JAIME CHAMBERLAIN, PRESIDENT, JC DISTRIBUTING INC.

Mr. CHAMBERLAIN. Chairwoman McSally and Representative Pearce, my name is Jaime Chamberlain. I am president of JC Distributing, a Nogales, Arizona-based company with a 46-year history of importing and distributing fresh produce from Mexico throughout the United States and Canada. I appreciate the opportunity to speak about my community and my industry as it pertains to border security.

For the last 29 years I have worked alongside with my family, our dedicated employees, and our grower partners to feed North America. This is a bold statement, but this is our mission and this is our passion. As a Nogales resident and as an American businessman, I believe that I bring a background and close to 3 decades of professional experience that allows me to assure you that my comments before you today are based on the realities of the border and the realities of North American trade and investment.

I am a big proponent of efforts and initiatives to promote trade and tourism in Southern Arizona for the benefit of my State and for my country. I am also an ardent proponent of enhanced security at our border's rural areas, as well as at our ports of entry. Let me assure you that these two positions are not contradictory but, in fact, they are essential and complementary.

---

[5] To see complete resolution and study guide go to *http://www.pcusa.org/site_media/media/uploads/acswp/pdf/immigration-resolution.pdf.*

The more effective and efficient that our enforcement agencies are at the border, the faster our produce, our manufactured goods, our cattle, our mining equipment, and our Mexican consumers can cross the border. With enhanced security our enforcement officials can, with greater certainty, secure our communities and bolster our economic productivity.

As a life-long border citizen, I feel it is my responsibility to articulate the truth about life on the border. We have distinct and unique physical security challenges all along our State, as many before me have testified to. But our businesses also require a safe and secure environment so that we may focus on the future of our economic viability. The stability of economic competitiveness strengthens our homeland against those who may want to disrupt our way of life.

Nogales, a community of 24,000 people, is the principal gateway for Arizona's trade and tourism with Mexico. As reported by the Federal Government, in 2015 Nogales processed 319,000 trucks, 3.5 million cars, and 10.5 million people. But I want to make sure that everyone understands that these are only northbound crossing statistics. When we add our southbound crossings, our numbers are staggering considering our small population. The reality is that our ports of entry at Nogales processed 640,000 trucks, 7 million cars, and 21 million people this past year alone.

These numbers represent more than $25 billion worth of imports and exports flowing through Nogales each year. And once you include Douglas and San Luis, these numbers easily exceed $30 billion worth of cross-border trade. It is also estimated that Mexican visitors spend over $7.3 million per day in Arizona. What happens at Nogales is important to Arizona and to the Nation.

Thanks to the efforts of many stakeholders in our community, among them the Greater Nogales Santa Cruz County Port Authority and the Fresh Produce Association of the Americas, close to $300 million have been invested in our community. Our commercial crossing has some of the shortest wait times of any comparable port of entry on the borders of Canada and Mexico. We have improved our situation in many ways over the last 10 years, but we still have much more that needs to be done.

These volumes can continue to grow but only if we provide Customs and Border Protection the necessary staffing, the newest technology for our equipment, and state-of-the-art facilities in order to do their job effectively and efficiently. Currently, CBP is doing the best they can protecting our interests with what they have. This is not acceptable for the citizens of Arizona, nor for the citizens of the United States of America. We can do better for those brave men and women in green and blue uniforms. We can do better for the businessmen and women working in our communities. We certainly can do better for our future citizens. This is the paradigm that I am asking you to change. The U.S. Government, combined with your leadership in Congress, needs to commit the necessary resources for our ports of entry. This is an urgent matter for our physical and for our economic security.

Securing the border at the border should be the strategy for our country. Unfortunately, many times when we ask for resources for our border, we are seen as a cost burden to the Nation. I don't know of a better use of our scarce Federal funds than investing in our sea ports, our land ports, and our air ports of entry. It needs to be seen, it must be seen as our best return on our investment for our Nation. By ensuring that our ports of entry are of the highest service standards for our foreign and domestic consumers, we would assure a more prosperous economic future for North America.

A new report from the research arm of the University of Southern California links Customs and Border Protection Officer staffing to both revenue generation and job creation. The National Center for Risk and Economic Analysis of Terrorism Events report released on April 8, 2013, estimates the impact of wait times at major ports of entry on the U.S. economy due to changes in CBP Officer staffing. The study concludes that adding one CBP Officer at one of the study's land or airport locations would inject $2 million into the economy and produce 33 new jobs. Yet our Nogales ports of entry are understaffed by almost 300 agents and over 20 canine units. We must keep our ports working at the speed of business. We have not done so in many years.

Efficient and well-staffed ports of entry mean foreign direct investment, it means job creation, it means higher-paying export-related jobs, and it means we can feel safe while conducting our business with our northern, our southern, and our global trade partners.

Madam Chairwoman and Members of the committee, I thank you for the opportunity to share some of my thoughts with you. Be assured of my personal commitment to working with you and the other stakeholders in this room to make our border a true asset for our economic and physical security. I think you can tell how passionate I am about these issues. There is simply too much at stake to approach this in any other way. I look forward to your questions.

[The prepared statement of Mr. Chamberlain follows:]

PREPARED STATEMENT OF JAIME CHAMBERLAIN

MAY 9, 2016

Chairwoman McSally and Members of the committee. My name is Jaime Chamberlain. I am president of JC Distributing Inc, a Nogales, Arizona based company with a 46-year history of importing and distributing fresh produce from Mexico throughout the United States and Canada. I appreciate the opportunity to speak about my community and my industry as it pertains to border security.

For the last 29 years I have worked alongside my family, our dedicated employees, and our grower partners to feed North America. This is a bold statement, but this our mission and our passion. As a Nogales resident and as an American businessman I believe that I bring a background, and close to 3 decades of professional experience, that allows me to assure you that my comments before you today are based on the realities of the border and the realities of North American trade and investment.

I am a big proponent of efforts and initiatives to promote trade and tourism in Southern Arizona for the benefit of my State and my country. I am also an ardent proponent of enhanced security at our borders rural areas as well as at our border ports of entry. Let me assure you that these 2 positions are not contradictory but in fact they are essential and complimentary.

The more effective and efficient that our enforcement agencies are at the border, the faster our produce, our manufactured goods, our cattle, our mining equipment, and our Mexican consumers can cross the border. With enhanced security our enforcement officials can, with greater certainty, secure our communities and bolster our economic productivity.

As a life-long Border Citizen, I feel it is my responsibility to articulate the truth about life on the border. We have distinct and unique physical security challenges all along our State as many before me have testified to. But our businesses also require a safe and secure environment so that we may focus on the future of our economic viability. The stability of economic competitiveness strengthens our homeland against those who may want to disrupt our way of life.

Nogales, a community of 24,000 people is the principal gateway for Arizona's trade and tourism with Mexico. As reported by the U.S. Federal Government, in 2015 Nogales processed 319,000 trucks, 3.5 million cars, and 10.5 million people. But I want to make sure that everyone understands that these are only north-bound crossing statistics. When we add our south-bound crossings, our numbers are staggering considering our small population. The reality is that our ports of entry at Nogales processed 640,000 trucks, 7 million cars, and 21 million people this past year.

These numbers represent more than $25 billion worth of imports and exports flowing through Nogales each year. And once you include Douglas and San Luis, these numbers easily exceed $30 billion worth of cross border trade. It is also estimated that Mexican visitors spend over $7.3 million per day in Arizona. What happens at Nogales is important to Arizona and the Nation.

Thanks to the efforts of many stakeholders in our community, among them the Greater Nogales Santa Cruz County Port Authority and the Fresh Produce Association of the Americas, close to $300 million have been invested in our community. Our commercial crossing has some of the shortest wait times of any comparable port of entry on the borders with Canada or Mexico. We have improved our situation in many ways in the past 10 years, but we still have much more that needs to be done.

These volumes can continue to grow but ONLY IF we provide Customs and Border Protection the necessary staffing, the newest technology for our equipment, and state-of-the-art facilities in order to do their job effectively and efficiently. Currently CBP is doing the best they can protecting our interests with what they have. This is not acceptable for the Citizens of Arizona, nor for the United States of America. We can do better for those brave men and women in green and blue uniforms. We can do better for the businessmen and women working in our communities. And we certainly should be better for our future citizens. This is the paradigm that I am asking you to change. The U.S. Government, combined with your leadership in Congress, needs to commit the necessary resources for our ports of entry. This is an urgent matter for our physical and our economic security.

Securing the border at the border should be the strategy for our country.

Unfortunately, many times when we ask for resources for our border, we are seen as a cost burden to the Nation. I don't know of a better use of our scarce Federal funds than investing in our sea ports, our land ports, and our air ports of entry. It needs to be seen, it must be seen as our best return on our investment for our Nation. By ensuring that our ports of entry are of the highest service standards for our foreign and domestic consumers, we would assure a more prosperous economic future for North America. Efficient and well-staffed ports of entry mean foreign direct investment, it means job creation, it means higher-paying export-related jobs, it means we can feel safe while conducting our business with our northern, our southern, and our global trade partners.

Madame Chair and Members of the committee, I thank you for the opportunity to share some of my thoughts with you. Be assured of my personal commitment of working with you and the other stakeholders in this room to make our border a true asset for our economic and physical security.

I think you can tell how passionate I am about these issues. There is simply too much at stake to approach this in any other way. I look forward to your questions.

Ms. MCSALLY. Great. Thank you, Mr. Chamberlain.

The Chair now recognizes Mrs. Stockholm Walden, please.

STATEMENT OF NAN STOCKHOLM WALDEN, VICE PRESIDENT AND LEGAL COUNSEL, FARMERS INVESTMENT CO. (FICO)

Ms. STOCKHOLM WALDEN. Thank you, Chair McSally and Representative Pearce. On behalf of Farmers Investment Company and the Green Valley Pecan Company, I am very grateful to be here this morning.

Just under 2 weeks ago, I had the opportunity to testify in Washington before the Oversight Subcommittee of the House Natural

Resources Committee on a similar topic, border security and Federal lands. My presence here today underscores how seriously we take these issues. My husband is in California today, but he certainly joins me in these remarks.

We were there with friends and local neighbors Sue and Jim Chilton, and our hearts go out to the Krentz family and to the Bell family, whom we know very well also, as to what they are undergoing on a daily basis.

Two percent of our population are farmers and ranchers, and they feed the world, not only this country but the world. You are part of that too, Jaime, and we are grateful and share many of your observations.

FICO is a major agricultural company founded almost 75 years ago by my father-in-law. Today, my husband and our 2 children are forming the third generation of Waldens, and we have many second- and third-generation workers, most of whom are of Mexican-American descent. We employ 260 full-time workers with full-time benefits, plus 50 to 60 seasonal workers during the harvest, which makes us one of the larger employers in Pima County.

We also have major farms in Cochise County at San Simone, about 3,500 acres of pecans for planting, a warehouse in Las Cruces, New Mexico. So I guess I represent several constituencies here. We are the largest integrated grower and processor of pecans in the world, and our pecans are known globally for their quality and value.

The FICO headquarters is located just over 40 miles north of the border off of I–19, and our home ranch is just less than 30 miles. We have a horse and cattle operation with 160 acres of private land and a 6,000-acre State grazing lease that straddles the southern part of Pima County and the northern part of the Santa Cruz County line just north of the checkpoint at I–19.

Our proximity to the border gives us first-hand experience with border security challenges, and we know the difficult job the Border Patrol is tasked to undertake. I have served on former Representative Gabby Giffords' Citizens Advisory Group on the I–19 checkpoint, and I would like to request that their recommendations be made part of the record because I think they are very apropos for today as well.

We would concur that we should secure the border at the border, and this is not because of some romantic notion we have about the difficulties that we are all facing but because we believe that too many alternate routes exist to get around the checkpoints. You gave the football analogy. Another one of my friends who played football, Gary Brasher, says it is sort of like standing in the middle of the field if you are the defense and hoping the quarterback will run into your arms.

We have a gas line and we have a dry riverbed. We have different transmission lines and a railroad that are all excellent routes to go around the checkpoint. So what happens is these people are flushed into our neighborhoods and ranches and communities, and the Border Patrol itself admits that 94 percent of the apprehensions are not made at the checkpoint but around it. So it is a serious concern.

I believe you have a military background. My husband was a pilot in Vietnam, flew the OV–1 Mohawk. This is a fanciful example, but if Mexico declared war on America, the Marines would not hold the line in Tucson or Phoenix. They would defend the border at the border, at our sovereign border. They would go into Mexico if necessary to push them back, and that is the same approach that we feel we need today.

We believe that comprehensive immigration reform is also essential for border security. This must be a multi-layered approach. We have to be smart about this, and I think Mayor Ortega and others that you heard on the first panel all mentioned this. Our visa system, our temporary worker system is broken. Agriculture, ranching, the hospitality industry, health care, construction, many of these industries depend upon a supply of entry-level and younger workers who will then be upwardly mobile, just as our ancestors were.

We also need seasonal workers. That benefits both of our countries.

I have personal experience and I have put in my longer testimony many, many episodes of high-speed chases by Border Patrol through, in one case, my front driveway, which I have detailed. Sharing some of these stories does not at all undermine the efforts of the Border Patrol. We are grateful for their service. Our ranch liaison, Jake Stukenberg, is doing a wonderful job, and I have called him at 11 o'clock at night when we had an incident on our ranch, and he is right there, and we really appreciate that.

However, following the recommendations that were part of the 9/11 report, we understand some of these have still not been implemented about communications, the ports of entry, and cracking down on employers, may I say, that hire people illegally. We were one of the first employers in Arizona to voluntarily use the e-Verify program, and we continue to do that with good results to this day. We don't appreciate other employers hiring people illegally because they undercut our wages and our benefits. We have had health benefits for our workers since the '50s. They are competing unfairly. We also drug-test all of our employees, including our management and including Dick and myself, on a random basis to cut down on the demand, which is what the sheriff was talking about in Cochise County.

It has to be a multi-layered strategy. It can't just be one thing.

The SCAP funding is also very important.

So again, I would be happy to go into this more with some specific recommendations that we have made. I also serve on the National Immigration Forum Board, which is a non-partisan group of people interested in a humane and enforceable immigration reform. We really appreciate your efforts to work together on a bipartisan basis. This is too important for any of us to play politics with. Thank you.

[The prepared statement of Ms. Stockholm Walden follows:]

MAY 9, 2016

INTRODUCTION

Chair McSally, I am Nan Stockholm Walden, vice president and counsel for Farmers Investment Co., (FICO), Farmers Water Co. (FWC) and The Green Valley Pecan Company here in Sahuarita, Arizona. I appreciate the opportunity to address you today on border security affecting our communities. A little over a week ago, I had to the opportunity to testify in Washington before the Subcommittee on Oversight and Investigations of the House Committee on Natural Resources on border security and my presence here today underscores how seriously we take these issues.

FICO is a major agricultural enterprise founded by my husband's father R. Keith Walden almost 75 years ago. Today, my husband, Dick Walden, who is the president and CEO of the company, and the third generation of Waldens, including daughter Deborah and son Rich, are active in the company.

We employ 260 permanent workers, many of whom also are second- and third-generation FICO employees, whom we consider family, as well. During harvest season, we hire an additional 50 to 60 workers, making us one of the larger employers in Pima County.

FICO is the largest integrated grower and processor of pecans in the world. We are also the largest producer of organic pecans. Research has shown that pecans are rich in antioxidants, can lower harmful LDL cholesterol, and contain 19 essential vitamins and minerals, as well as being an excellent source of protein. FICO sells pecans to food makers including makers of cereals, health bars, ice creams, candies, and bakery goods, to retail chains that package our nuts under their label, and directly to customers—both here and abroad. We also buy pecans from other growers in the United States and Mexico.

FICO owns approximately 11,000 acres in Southern Arizona, of which about 7,500 acres are irrigated and under cultivation for pecan nuts, a tree native to North America.

The FICO headquarters is located here in Sahuarita just over 40 miles north of the border, and our home ranch is just less than 30 miles. Our property in Amado is a horse and cattle operation that includes 160 acres of private land and a 6,000-acre State grazing lease.

Consequently, we have the first-hand experience with border security challenges, and we know the difficult job the Border Patrol is tasked to undertake. The Border Patrol has responded to calls on both our farm and our ranch. I might add that our Border Patrol Tucson Sector Ranch Liaison, Jake Stukenberg, does an excellent job helping us cooperate with Border Patrol.

I also serve on the board of directors of the National Immigration Forum, a nonpartisan organization that works with diverse constituencies especially business, faith, and law enforcement leaders advocating for immigrants and responsible immigration policy. This policy must reflect immigrants' contributions to our Nation's history, culture, and growth, and their continuing contributions to our country's economy, especially in the agriculture and ranching sectors in rural communities.

The views I am offering today are informed by this context.

IMPACT OF PERMANENT BORDER CHECKPOINTS ON OUR COMMUNITIES

FICO has long-standing concerns about the effectiveness of permanent Border Patrol checkpoints and their impacts on the surrounding community including nearby public lands. We met often with your predecessors including former Rep. Jim Kolbe, and I served on Rep. Gabrielle Giffords' Citizens' Advisory Committee on Checkpoints.

Those of us that live in areas surrounding the checkpoint have, for years, been exposed to the degradation of our public safety because of them—high-speed car chases through our neighborhoods, gunshot victims, and the like. I have experienced a high-speed chase by Border Patrol through my front driveway in Sahuarita, AZ that I am sure would have killed an employee or me had I not been in my home office at the time. The result was that a couple and 2 young terrified kids were apprehended, but there were no weapons or drugs found in their car.

My neighbor at the Agua Linda Ranch was pushed down on the ground by Border Patrol Agents around 10 p.m., one night when he was near his ranch house, changing the irrigation set on his vegetables, dressed in his pajamas, despite the fact that he identified himself as the owner of the property.

Our neighbors and ourselves have had many similar experiences of livestock buzzed by helicopters flying too low over pastures, gates left open, fences cut, and crossers asked to dump all their belongings on our property, which were left there, not confiscated. We have had numerous examples of Border Patrol Agents being unfamiliar or lost on our ranch property, which is within a quarter mile of the major North/South Interstate, I–19.

A senior member of our team who happens to be Mexican-American was stopped by the Border Patrol 40 miles north of the border on her way from her home to work. She was driving a late model SUV with 2 young daughters in the back in car seats. When she asked why she was stopped, the Border Patrol Officer replied, "You fit the profile."

"What profile is that?" she asked.

"Driving a late model SUV and obeying the traffic laws and speed limit," was the reply.

Sharing these stories with you does not at all mean we do not appreciate the efforts of the Border Patrol. Rather, proper training is crucial to Border Patrol Agents working successfully with rural communities. We have noted that because Border Patrol has significantly increased staffing levels in recent years, there is a lot of transferring agents from one sector to another, high rates of turnover, and lack of uniform training.

The Border Patrol strategy, "Defense-in-Depth," calls for retreating 30 or so miles from the border with fixed checkpoints. This strategy has us living in a no man's land and underestimates the intelligence of the enemy we are fighting—the drug and human smugglers. The assumption that these criminals will not circumvent fixed checkpoints and traverse through our neighborhoods, our ranches, our communities, and our public lands is not based in reality.

There have been several in-depth examinations of the effectiveness and impacts of the Border Patrols checkpoint strategy.

GAO, August 2009[1].—This GAO report confirmed that the Border Patrol was proceeding without adequate information on the effectiveness of fixed checkpoints and their adverse impacts on the public safety and quality of life of southern Arizona. GAO found that there were "information gaps and reporting issues" because of insufficient data, the agency was unable to compare the cost-effectiveness of checkpoints to other strategies, and the Border Patrol had misrepresented its checkpoint performance. It also found that of all the apprehensions of illegal immigrants in the vicinity of the I–19 checkpoint in a certain fiscal year, "94% occurred in the areas surrounding the checkpoint, while only 6% took place at the checkpoint itself." In other words, these statistics make it clear that the checkpoint was driving criminal activities into the areas surrounding the checkpoint.

Udall Center for Studies in Public Policy, the University of Arizona, December 2012[2].—After undertaking a detailed statistical analysis this study found that the I–19 checkpoint is having a significant impact on the property values of the community surrounding this facility. This means that rural communities in the vicinity of the checkpoint, like Tubac, Arizona, are bearing a disproportionate economic burden for this border security tactic.

Tubac is in a rural area 20 miles from the border. It has become a major draw for tourists and businesses due to its historical, cultural, artistic, and recreational facilities. Yet we know of many visitors and potential residents who have cancelled vacations or real estate purchases due to concerns about the permanent checkpoint and appearance of extreme militarism in the area. According to the Arizona Office of Tourism, tourism spending generates $3.6 billion in economic activity annually and employs over 30,000 individuals in southern Arizona.[3] The economic impacts of border security measures must be carefully considered.

---

[1] United States, Government Accountability Office (GAO). (2009). *Checkpoints Contribute to Border Patrol's Mission, but More Consistent Data Collection and Performance Measurement Could Improve Effectiveness* (GAO–09–824). Washington, District of Columbia.

[2] Gans, J., M.S., M.P. (December 2012). *The Border Patrol Checkpoint on Interstate 19 in Southern Arizona: A Case Study of Impacts on Residential Real Estate* (Rep.). Udall Center for Studies in Public Policy, The University of Arizona.

[3] Arizona Travel Impacts 1998–2014p. (2015, June). Retrieved from *https://tourism.az.gov/sites/default/files/documents/files/AZImp14pFinal_1.pdf*. Report prepared by Dean Runyon & Associates.

GAO, December 2012[4].—This report found, among other things, that because of data limitations the Border Patrol is unable to compare the effectiveness how resources are deployed among sectors. Each sector collects and reports the data differently thus precluding comparison. Policymakers and Border Patrol leadership are unable to effectively assess the effectiveness of tactics such as the checkpoint.

The information in a report issued last month by the Congressional Research Service (CRS) is also worth considering. In it, CRS noted discussed unintended and secondary consequences of border enforcement on border-area crime, migrant flow and migrants deaths, environmental impacts, effects on border communities, and U.S. foreign relations. Importantly, the report explains that an "unintended consequence of enhanced border enforcement between ports of entry may have been an increase in unauthorized entries through ports of entry and other means." Specifically, the report found that "based on three different surveys conducted between 2008 and 2010, UCSD researchers found that the probability of being apprehended while passing through a port of entry without authorization was about half as high as the probability of being apprehended while crossing between the ports."[5] While the report does not specifically address interior checkpoints, its findings raise yet again the question of whether resources would be better shifted to border ports of entry.

FICO believes that fixed permanent checkpoints threaten public safety in addition to resulting in significant economic consequences. It is clear in our view that they drive illegal activities away from the checkpoint into surrounding areas including Federal public lands. We strongly believe that the border should be secured at the border.

COMPREHENSIVE IMMIGRATION REFORM

As long-time business owners who live and work within 30 to 40 miles of the border, I cannot emphasize enough the inexorable link between border security and comprehensive immigration reform.

We understand the gravity of the border situation—the drug-associated violence, human smuggling, and environmental impacts—as well as the impacts of some enforcement activities on our commerce and property values.

We also know the effects of poorly crafted or implemented Federal or State policies that create a climate of fear and discrimination among the civilian population—business and commerce decline and families suffer.

That makes your job all the more challenging and important—and we thank you for hearing from the people like us who live this situation daily, and for those of you who have visited the border and talked to residents and those who work and travel on both sides of the line.

In 2008, I testified before the House Subcommittee on Homeland Security, regarding the importance of comprehensive immigration reform. Much of what I said in 2008 remains a problem today.

We must remember and appreciate the contributions of our legal immigrants and those in our area who are of Mexican-American descent, without whom agriculture and ranching could not flourish in the United States. The health care industry, restaurant and hospitality industry, construction, mining, and many other sectors depend on continued renewal of both entry-level and skilled labor from other countries.

Mexico is our third-largest trading partner, behind Canada and China. The United States and Mexican economies are interdependent. As Mexico strengthens its institutions and economy, the benefits flow into our country, and there is less pressure for illegal migration.

In our experience, the paths for both permanent and temporary legal workers in the United States are long, crooked, and in some cases dead-ends. Since 1986 we have not uniformly enforced immigration laws, nor have we adequately dealt with ways to efficiently permit temporary workers, and provide a timely path to citizenship for those who merit it. Agricultural and other visa programs are impractical and unworkable.

---

[4] Government Accountability Office (GAO). (2012). *Key Elements of New Strategic Plan Not Yet in Place to Inform Border Security Status and Resource Needs* (GAO–13–25). Washington, District of Columbia.

[5] "Border Security: Immigration Enforcement Between Ports of Entry", Carla N. Argueta, Congressional Research Service, April 19, 2016.

Polls show that most Americans favor comprehensive immigration reform, including a path to citizenship and that these levels of support have remained constant for more than a decade.[6]

National security experts under both Republican and Democratic administrations,[7] assert that the most effective border security strategy is comprehensive immigration reform. We must fix the immigration system by providing legal avenues for workers to enter the United States when needed and allow families to reunify. The 1986 Immigration Reform and Control Act, which resolved the status of most undocumented immigrants at the time, did not adequately address the demand for legal immigrant labor. Because there continues to be a demand for immigrant labor, individuals from other countries who seek a better life are drawn to our Nation that is full of opportunity.

By providing more avenues for these individuals to come to the United States through legal means, law enforcement and border officials will be able to spend fewer resources toward immigrants migrating for economic reasons and more resources toward genuine criminal and terrorist threats that could harm our communities. Smart enforcement and border security, coupled with comprehensive immigration reforms, can improve border security.

CONCLUSION

We appreciate the professional efforts of the Border Patrol and we certainly believe in securing our Nation's borders, preferably at the border or in the immediate vicinity.

Congress should also enact comprehensive immigration reform that addresses our society's need for lawful immigrants, and, at the same time protects and enhances the public lands our growing population needs for recreational, economic, and spiritual needs.

Ms. MCSALLY. Thank you, Ms. Walden.

The Chair now recognizes Mr. Krentz.

STATEMENT OF FRANK KRENTZ, RANCHER

Mr. KRENTZ. Chairwoman McSally and Mr. Pearce, thank you for coming down here today. My name is Frank Krentz. I am a fifth-generation rancher in Cochise County on the same piece of ground that my forefathers started 109 years ago.

Almost 6 years ago one morning my cousin, my uncle, my father, and myself sat down for breakfast and talked about what we were going to do for the day. When we finished my cousin and I went to move cows while my father went to check a motor and my other uncle went to look at other waters on the ranch. That was the last time I saw my father. Rob Krentz was on his way to check the motor when he called his brother on the cell phone and said there was someone walking across the pasture and was going to go see what was going on.

Friends and neighbors came to help us look for my father when we couldn't get a hold of him for hours. A neighbor called the sheriff's search and rescue team and they started looking as well. The news came in late that night that they had found my father.

Rob was a great and caring man, helpful to others and dedicated to the way of life that he loved. He worked to help others, volunteering his time to help the local school, community, family, and friends.

---

[6] *In United States, 65% Favor Path to Citizenship for Illegal Immigrants.* (2015, August 12). Retrieved April 26, 2016, *from http://www.gallup.com/poll/184577/favor-path-citizenship-illegal-immigrants.aspx.*

[7] Molnar, P. (2013, April 8). *Panetta Lecture Series: Border security experts say immigration reform is vital.* Retrieved April 26, 2016, from *http://www.santacruzsentinel.com/article/zz/20130408/NEWS/130408557.*

To understand where I am coming from, you need to know the people that live in this area. Most of the people in this part of the world have had at least one incident that has involved problems with people trespassing across from the Southern Border illegally. When I was younger we would see people crossing the border and knew that they were running from problems worse than getting caught on the northern side. Knowing that the Arizona desert can be dangerous to cross, we would make sure that there would be Border Patrol on the way to help them. I can remember a time in 1999 I saw two different groups of people crossing the ranch that numbered larger than 100. We used to approach these people as Christians to make sure that there were no injuries and tell them that Border Patrol would be here shortly to help them. We would always do this even after we had had our houses broken into, our vehicles stolen, trash left in the country, and water lines broken. There have been many times when we would go and check storage tanks that we would spend a week's worth of time to make full be drained because illegals would break water lines or floats to get a drink of water and draining thousands of gallons of water out on the ground. We would still try our best to give these people help.

After losing my father, all of that changed. Now we don't go near these people. Not knowing what the situation holds, we don't put ourselves in a position that would get us into trouble. The people we see now are not the large groups fleeing but the small groups packing drugs. There have been pictures taken of these small groups armed as well.

I was told once by a U.S. Congressman that the people along the border have become numb to the whole border issue, that we have gotten used to the idea that this is the new normal if we want to live here. I wouldn't say that we have become numb, but we have become resilient, that we want to live in this part of the world, that many of the families around have been here for many years and generations and hope to have many more generations in this part of the country they have carved out for themselves.

People who aren't from here get shocked when I tell them the problems we face on a daily basis. They ask why don't you move away from there? It is hard for some people to know what 100 years of working in one place can look like. I am a fifth-generation rancher and feel a sense of pride of what I am doing, raising livestock for our Nation, being out in the country and working in a business sector that less than 2 percent of the country are able to do.

As our guests leave here today, I would like you to take with you the gratitude from me and my friends and family for hearing what we have gone through, to go back and say that there is a problem that needs more attention.

Before I close and I have a little bit of time, I would like noted in the record some other issues that need to be held up. Ever since I was a little kid, one of our family friends, Gary Thrasher, the local in the area, and I am sure you all have met him before, he has always voiced to me that one of the major issues that is seen in rural agriculture is disease that can be easily transported across the border. My great uncle in the '40s and '50s fought back tuberculosis and hoof and mouth out of the United States, and fought it into Sonora, Mexico, into Chihuahua, Mexico, and fought it deep down south. The Mexican government has been doing good work trying to regulate that disease and the health of the animals to keep it away from our borders, because once that does get into our Nation's food supply, it can be very detrimental. It can eradicate whole herds in whole counties. It can be that fast-spreading.

Another issue that I would like you to be aware of is what Mr. Ortega was saying about how the population has decreased over the last number of years. It has also affected the land values. I have had a neighboring rancher that has recently had to have his ranch appraised for a business organization, and he says in the last 15 years his ranch has lost half of its value just because of the location to the border.

When you go back, I would like you to heed that there are issues that are addressed and that securing the border is not just not allowing anybody in but it is controlling what can come in and making it a manageable factor because, with a simple ranching analogy, if you run too many cows, you are going to run out of grass, and then you are not going to be able to run any. So I would like you to go back and thank you for listening to us today. Thank you.

[The prepared statement of Mr. Krentz follows:]

PREPARED STATEMENT OF FRANK KRENTZ

MAY 9, 2016

Almost 6 years ago one morning my cousin, my uncle, my father, and myself sat down for breakfast and talked about what we were going to do for the day. When we finished my cousin and I went to move cows while my father went to check a motor and my uncle went to check other waters on the ranch. That was the last time I saw my father. Rob Krentz was on his way to check the motor when he called his brother on the cell phone and said there was someone walking across the pasture and was going to see what was going on.

Friend and neighbors came to help us look for my father when we couldn't get a hold of him for hours. A neighbor called the sheriff's search-and-rescue team and they started looking. The news came in late that night that they had found my father.

Rob was a great and caring man. Helpful to others and dedicated to the way of life that he loved. He worked to help others volunteering his time to help the local school, his community, and friends and family.

To understand where I am coming from you need to know the people that live in this area. Most of the people in this part of the world has had at least one incident that involved problems with people trespassing across the Southern Border illegally. When I was younger we would see people crossing the border and knew that they were running from problems worse than getting caught on the northern side. Knowing that the Arizona desert can be dangerous to cross we would make sure there would be Border Patrol on the way to help them. I can remember a time in 1999 I saw 2 different groups of people crossing the ranch that numbered larger than 100. We used to approach these people as Christians to make sure there were no injuries and tell them that Border Patrol would be here shortly to help them. We would always do this even after we have had our houses broken into, vehicles stolen, trash left in the country, and waters broken. There have been many times when we would go and check storage tanks that we would spent a week's worth of time to make full be drained because illegals would break water lines or floats to get a drink of water and draining thousands of gallons of water out on the ground. And we would still try our best to get these people help.

After losing my father all of that changed. Now we don't go near these people. Not knowing what the situation holds we don't put ourselves in a position that would get us into trouble. The people that we see now are not the large groups of people fleeing but small groups packing drugs. There have been pictures taken of some of these small groups armed as well.

I was told once by a U.S. Congressman that the people along the border has become "NUMB" to the whole border issue. They have gotten used to the idea that this is the new normal if they want to live here. I wouldn't say that we have become "NUMB" but we have become resilient; that we want to live in this part of the world, that many of the families here have been here for many years and generations and hope to have many more on this part of the world they have carved out for themselves.

People who aren't from here get shocked when I tell them the problems we face on a daily basis. They ask why don't you move away from there? It is hard for some people to know what 100 years of working in one place can look like. I am fifth generation on the ranch and feel a sense of pride of what I am doing raising livestock for our Nation. Being out in the country and working in a business sector that is less than 1% of the country are able to do.

As our guest leave here today I would like you to take with you the gratitude from me and my friends and family for hearing what we are going through. To go back and say that there is a problem that needs more attention than what is given to it. Finally, that we work hard to stay in this country that we live in and we want to be able to continue to live and work free of fear of what would happen if we were to leave our house to go to work.

Ms. McSALLY. Thank you, Mr. Krentz. I have to say for myself and Mr. Pearce, our hearts continue to be with your family. You know personally the price that you paid every day, the loss of your dad from an unsecure border. I really appreciate you coming and sharing your perspective today.

I want to thank you for the diversity and the perspectives of the whole panel.

I want to start with a similar question I asked the first panel, which is—well, part of it is what trends have you seen over the last decade, shifting really from potentially more people coming to find work versus hardened cartels that are now controlling traffic that have become far more dangerous?

What do you want Washington, DC and others—what do you want in the record besides what you just said, the trends that have changed over the years? What do you need them to hear from you and your perspectives about what is going on in our communities? If the President were standing before you today and you are the new Secretary of Homeland Security and you are in charge of now securing the border, it is your strategy, it is your ideas, you are resource unconstrained, from each of your perspectives what would that look like? What would you do in order to address these issues that you have all very eloquently brought to our attention today?

Starting with Mr. Bell.

Mr. BELL. Well, I think I would start with what my main point was, actually getting access to the border. The previous panel talked about the wilderness areas and things of that nature that prevent access and prevent sometimes the ability to patrol the border if there is an actual pursuit going on. There are MOUs in place.

But a lot of our ranch is on Federal land, and there is a big process that needs to be gone through to get roads put in. We just had a 2-mile stretch of road put in along the border, as close to the border as you could get it, because the terrain is very, very difficult. So they were able to get it as close to the border as possible, but that process took more than a decade to get done, and most of it, because of the required permitting and everything else to get it okayed, to get it done, it took about 4 years to construct, and they are just finishing it up right now, and it is 2 miles. But it has made a difference.

Technology has made a difference, but it is only in a limited space, like I told you. We need to keep that progress and keep it going.

So for me, it is getting the access, getting to a place where we can defend, and then having the resources to back it up, because there is no silver bullet. It is not just that one thing. We need everything. We need boots on the ground. We need consequences. We need air support. We need everything to get it done because there is not one key you can stick in that is going to stop it. You need to have a myriad of things to do that.

Ms. McSALLY. Thanks.

Mr. Adams.

Mr. ADAMS. Thank you. One of the huge trends that has changed are the types of folks that we encounter in the Migrant Resource Center. Our ministry began 10 years ago having what is called the Migrant Resource Center on the south side of the border, and we have received over 86,000 men, women, and children who have been returned to Mexico from the United States by our U.S. Border Patrol.

Early in that time, there were lots of folks who were crossing for the first time, going for job purposes, things like that. One of the things we have seen dramatically in the last piece is the number of people who are returning to the United States, not going for the first time, usually going to be reunited with families in the United States. There is 1 woman I mentioned in my written testimony, Hermina, who has lived in South Carolina for over 10 years, and she ended up in the Center, has a 6-year-old son who was born in South Carolina, and she returned to Mexico to see her dying father. She talked about being caught between two worlds. She said just pray for us, pray.

So that is a reality that we are seeing, is more folks, especially from Mexico—there is not as much economic migration, but the folks who are returning from Mexico tend to be folks returning. So that is a big trend.

The other trend that we saw at our prayer vigil—every Tuesday we have a prayer vigil for those who died crossing into the United States, and one of the things that we began seeing in the early 2000s is more and more women showing up on the crosses that were there. This is going back a little bit historically, but there was a shift from mainly young men crossing the border to women crossing the border.

One of our partners in Colorado, we were up visiting there and they took us to a place where they just have migrant housing. It had been a big kind of bunkhouse, and it had been changed into townhouses. So we asked them what has changed, and they said now families are coming, women are coming.

So one of the ironies of our border security policy of the '90s is that in many ways we did a better job of keeping people in the country as opposed to out of the country, because it changed historic patterns of migrating for 5 years or so, going back every year. As it became harder and more expensive and more dangerous to return home between seasons, people stayed. Once that happened, and I have personally had families struggle with this, what do you do with separated families? So more women have gone.

Unfortunately, there is a higher percentage of women dying as opposed to their numbers than men, and that is something we have seen as well there.

A trend that we haven't seen change is the percentage of death happening in crossing, even as the number of people crossing has gone down. The percentage per crossing of people dying has actually maintained the same or increased a little bit. So that is a disturbing change that has not changed and needs to change.

Then the second piece that hasn't changed that needs to change is the dichotomy between security and immigration reform. I think that is a very false dichotomy, and it is a very dangerous dichotomy, because we have been hearing it for 20 years. It seems like a simple thing to me, and maybe it is not, but it seems like if we take folks who are coming for economic reasons or for family reasons, like many of our ancestors had come in the past, and look at the economic realities on both sides of our borders, and we provide for safe and efficient ways for folks to come through ports of entry, then it would be a lot easier for our law enforcement to be able to detect folks who are coming with ill intent.

So I think we need to change that trend, and you can be one of the persons to change that trend, to say that is a false dichotomy and it needs to change, because if it doesn't change, we are not going to have a secure border and we are going to continue to increase the number of people who die trying to reach the American Dream.

Ms. MCSALLY. Thank you.

Mr. CHAMBERLAIN. Chairwoman McSally, if I had an unlimited amount of resources, there are a ton of things I would do, and if I had the President in front of me I would say a whole lot of things. One of the things that is most important to us and what I testified to is toward the efficient and expedient flow of commerce between the ports of entry. That is extremely important for us in Nogales, Arizona.

One of the things that is bothersome is that within the Department of Homeland Security structure you have Border Patrol, which is funded by direct appropriations, and you have Customs that is partially funded by user fees and direct appropriations. I think that is an issue that needs to be addressed. It shouldn't be an either/or issue. I think commerce is just as important as what happens in the rural areas of the United States. I have a tremendous amount of respect for the ranchers and for the rural areas of Arizona. I have a great relationship with Dan Bell. We happen to be neighbors and growing up as kids, and I understand their issues. Even the agent Del Cueto said the agencies did not grow in the same way in the last 10 years, 10 to 15 years.

I think that as we strengthened between our ports of entry in the rural areas where we grew the Border Patrol, I think we had a tough time growing Customs, and therefore many more ports of entry became porous. As you can see from the terrorists from 9/11, they all came through a port of entry, whether it was a sea port, a land port, or an airport. They didn't come through the desert. That doesn't mean that that can't happen in the future. But our ports of entry, I believe, are just as important, and they are just as dangerous.

You have the Port of Nogales that catches as much drugs as any 5 ports on the southern border of Texas. So that is extremely dangerous, and it is only escalating. It is also dangerous to have an understaffed port of entry. You have agents on the border that are working 16-hour shifts and they have very, very little time to determine what is in front of them. When they have a car that comes in front of them or a pedestrian that crosses right in front of them, they have very little time to examine them and figure out exactly if they are coming for legitimate trade and legitimate purposes or for illegal purposes.

So I think that that is one of the things that I would ask you all to change. When I ask you to change the paradigm, that is one of them.

Mr. Del Cueto also says that the metrics in which the statistics are given are probably not true. I tend to believe him. I think that we should be able to have a much better metrics. But that also applies to our ports of entry. It is not only in our rural areas where we have figures and statistics that are not correct but it is also at our ports of entry.

When we say in Washington that our ports of entry are secure, that is not correct. If we are getting the amount of drugs and illegal contraband, whether it is counterfeit money or counterfeit Levi's or counterfeit shoes or whatever it may be, or even southbound with illegal proceeds or weapons and bullets that are found in our southbound inspections, then we have just as much of a danger there as we do in the rural areas.

But let me be clear: This is not an either/or thing. I believe the Federal Government can do both things at the same time. Securing Danny Bell's ranch and securing Jaime Chamberlain's port of entry are extremely important, but they are not just our situations. They are all our country's situation, and they are definitely an issue for the State of Arizona.

We tend to be looked over when the strategy comes into place. I really, really thank you all for allowing us to testify in front of you, to have a voice in Washington, DC so that you can convey what we feel every single day. This is something that has been lacking for the State of Arizona for many, many years. Finally, we have a seat at the table. Hopefully we are going to be heard. Thank you.

Ms. McSALLY. Thank you, Mr. Chamberlain.

Before we go on to Ms. Walden, I just want to reiterate the importance of many of the issues that you raised at our ports of entry. Again, we were focusing on the rural areas between the ports, but we have to chew gum and walk at the same time. We have to be able to do both of these. These are vitally important. For those who are in the audience and didn't tune in to our last hearing, this is something that is impacting us from a security and an economic point of view in Arizona and across the country.

I am proud to say my first bill passed into law is the Border Jobs for Veterans Act, which is intended to address some of these shortage issues. It takes 18 months for someone to be hired for one of these critical positions at our ports of entry, 18 months. You said we should be moving at the speed of business. It is moving at the speed of bureaucracy, and nobody can wait for 18 months to get a job. While we need to vet them, this is just unsatisfactory, and we are going to continue to hammer and do what we can in order to speed up this time line for those that are veterans and others that are looking for these jobs that are critical.

This next week in Congress we are going to be voting on a number of bills related to the opioid tragedy that is happening across our country. We have an epidemic of those that are addicted and dying from opioid abuse. This is like we have not seen in my lifetime, these last few years, and the price of drugs, the price of opioids is still cheap. So we have a long way to go to be able to address this issue, and it is literally causing the deaths of the sons and daughters in our community, and we have to address this in a very holistic approach as well.

So I just wanted to comment on that and hand it to Ms. Walden.

Ms. STOCKHOLM WALDEN. Thank you. As you can see, there is more that we agree on than we disagree on, and sometimes we find it very hard to understand why our representatives in Washington can't sit down and reason together on such vital issues.

I would like to echo really what everyone has said so far. You know, we are confusing Juan, or Juanita as the pastor pointed out, who just wants to come here and work, maybe seasonally or maybe earn a legal path to citizenship, with Juan the drug smuggler, and that is the big problem. Border Patrol, speaking off the record when we talk to them on our ranches and farms they will say, you know, right now I am looking for a needle in a haystack. My haystack is too big. I have all these people lumped into the same category. If there could be a way to differentiate so I could really focus on the terrorists and the drug smugglers and the human smugglers and the people that mean our country harm and, frankly, harm to Mexico as well, that would make my job so much easier. Which is why, again, I agree so much with what Jaime Chamberlain just said about the need to do immigration reform hand-in-hand.

If we had an I.D. card with a biometric marker, if we had a reasonable path to citizenship, or at least a temporary worker permit so they could work here while they are trying to become citizens if they are eligible, it would cut out the underground economy. They would pay taxes. They would pay into Social Security. We would eliminate the employers who are abusing them. We would eliminate people being afraid to report criminal activity or domestic violence. We would eliminate all these hardships on these families who might have some members who are legal. The children might be legal but maybe the grandfather or one of the parents is not legal.

It is just tearing this country apart. Let's remember for a minute, this was Mexico where we are sitting up until recent times, and we still have families that live and work on both sides of the line, that own ranches and farms on both sides of the line. We source pecans from Mexico. Our countries and our cultures are so integrated here, and this is true of the Native American people too, by the way, who live on both sides of what is currently the border.

So we also, I think, need to realize that the Border Patrol and this new organization under Homeland Security is relatively new. It doesn't have the checks and balances of our military. Frankly, I don't believe it has the strategic capabilities of our military in many ways. The training, the lack of metrics—I think both GAO and the University of Arizona Udall Center and some other studies that have been done show that the Border Patrol isn't keeping statistics correctly and accurately, the way that we do in the Armed Forces, for example, and I think this is very important.

So I think anything that can be done organizationally, anything that can be done to increase the training of a lot of these young agents—frankly, it is not just more boots on the ground, but it is the training and the coordination and their work with local law enforcement. That is really what is going to make them successful in their missions in the field.

Then from all standpoints, one of the groups—I serve on the board of the National Immigration Forum. It has formed the Bibles, Badges, and Business Coalition. These are people from the faith community, from law enforcement, and from the business community. We all agree on the problems here, and at least on some of the solutions.

So again, we are grateful for you being here today and gathering the information first-hand, and certainly also your efforts on the drug treatment. We have to have on-demand treatment. We have to recognize that this drug pandemic is like a war. It is wiping out a generation of Americans. It is leaving others impaired forever. They are going to be a huge burden on our society, and it is a huge loss of the best and the brightest that are going to be our future leaders. So we commend you on your work on that as well.

Ms. MCSALLY. Thank you, Ms. Walden.

Mr. Krentz.

Mr. KRENTZ. Being the last one on the panel, I could say I concur and I would be fine.

[Laughter.]

Ms. MCSALLY. We will start with you on the next round.

Mr. KRENTZ. Right.

You build a 12-foot wall, somebody is going to build a 13-foot ladder. You build a 50-foot-wide wall, somebody is going to dig a half-mile tunnel. I don't think a wall is the end-all answer. Half the border isn't secured with a wall because of terrain. It is just that difficult to put in.

There are current laws and regulations on the books that are very valid and very feasible. The people that are on the ground, the Border Patrol, the sheriff departments—the sheriff departments are a lot more agile on accessing their laws so that they can prosecute perpetrators than the Border Patrol has. If there was a better way for the Border Patrol to be able to do what they are able to do and capable of but not able to do, that would solve a lot of the situation.

An easier way for people to get a direct visa. If somebody wants to come to this country—my grandfather, prior to the Vecera Program, worked people and helped them into citizenship, and if you want to find somebody that is more aggravated with illegal immigration, go talk to those gentlemen that are now productive members of society in America and are proud to be here that worked through the proper system. They are very aggravated with people who are taking advantage of the system.

If there was an easier way for them, for the people that want to be in here to be in here, that would make our illegal crossing and the deaths across the arid Arizona and New Mexico regions a lot less of an issue.

One of the other things is the circuit courts. Why do we hear of people who are crossing the border ask, when they get caught by Border Patrol, where am I at? Am I in Arizona in the 9th Circuit, or am I in New Mexico in the 8th Circuit? That is all on the leniency of the court system. The further west you go, the more lenient you are on issues like that. I know those are kind of taboo types of subjects, but that is what is happening out here.

If you could address some of those issues, you could probably get ahead. If you add unlimited funds to solve the situation, a simple rancher analogy: Make that side of the fence better than your side so that people want to stay home. You have to get rid of the hierarchy that is entrenched into the society. But that is something that has been that way for many, many, many, many, many years.

But I believe if you could start letting the Border Patrol do what they are capable of, and then the way the judicial system is set up, you would have a pretty good start. There is no reason to start new laws when some of the ones that are here already work. Thank you.

Ms. McSally. Thank you, Mr. Krentz.

Before I hand it over to Mr. Pearce, I am always trying to look for where we can find agreement, so I just want to rephrase what I think I heard, although there are some different perspectives from the whole panel. This is not intended to be about immigration reform as its main focus, but I think everyone on the panel—there may be great disagreement on what to do with those who are here illegally, and we could debate that for the rest of the day, but I think everybody here agrees that we need a legal immigration system that actually allows for people to come over and spend money for the day, come shop at our malls and come through the ports of entry in a way that they are vetted and able to either shop or work temporarily in positions that are going to grow our economy.

We can't accept everybody. We can't. But there has to be a better system right now. It is cumbersome. It takes too long. It is confusing. It is based on random country quotas that allow people to come through the turnstile that are actually going to help our economy, not hurt our economy. So there needs to be a revamping and a modernizing of the legal immigration system. Is that a fair statement that everyone on the panel agrees to? I just want to hear a yes out of everybody.

Mr. Bell.

Mr. Bell. Yes.

Mr. Adams. Pastor Adams.

Mr. Adams. Yes.

Ms. Stockholm Walden. Yes.

Ms. McSally. Jaime.

Mr. Chamberlain. Yes.

Ms. McSally. Okay. Great. We found another area that generally, again—how that happens is a lot of devils in the details, but addressing that particular issue so that we can focus on the transnational criminal organizations. Again, there are still some challenges moving forward with all of this, but I just wanted to find those areas of agreement.

Now I will hand it over to Mr. Pearce.

Mr. PEARCE. Thank you, Madam Chair.

Just following up on that agreement, there is actually down in the trenches in the back rows much more agreement between the parties. The differences come as it moves towards leadership. The leadership in both parties have agreements and hooks or whatever. That is just the truth of the matter.

Beto O'Rourke out of El Paso, he and I worked on a couple of bills, and we felt like we should show that Democrats and Republicans are working together. Then we said we ought to go at the hardest issue, and that is immigration. So we have a couple of bills that are very limited, but I think if we would start taking limited solutions to pieces of the problem, we could start unraveling it. But many in Washington just refuse any single attempts and efforts. That is one reason the system bogs down.

Mr. Chamberlain, I appreciate your passion about business. Again as a business person, that is something I can identify with. But I will tell you from my perspective on this side of the table that when we increase the assets, we don't usually see much change, and it gets very frustrating. So we increased the Border Patrol by double back under President Bush, but in the last 10 years, from 2005 to 2015, Customs has gone up double, from about $5 billion to $10 billion, and I am hearing that it hasn't changed any.

So, did you want to say something? Then to the whole idea of technology, right now we have towers and cameras going up. Mr. Bell, you mentioned those. But a decade ago we put $200 million into a system that was supposed to be computers, towers, and cameras, and we did not, the whole border did not get one functioning system. Some have towers and no computers, some had cameras and no towers, some had computers and no towers or cameras, and you get very frustrated with an agency that will squander $200 million, that will squander everything you put in.

So it is a very frustrating thing to hear that the money we are channeling into Customs—not Border Patrol; that is different. So the money we are channeling to Customs, it never feeds down to here. We lobbied and got a new border crossing at one of the towns in our district, and then again they started saying the day after they built it, well, it should have had a truck lane and it doesn't.

You know, you just sit here and you say you built the thing from new and you designed it, not Congress.

Go ahead, sir.

Mr. CHAMBERLAIN. You are correct, and I am very frustrated. We worked very diligently in Nogales, Arizona, and there were many stakeholders that worked diligently on the building and the remodeling of the Mariposa port of entry. It was a tremendous feat and we were extremely fortunate that there was stimulus money and that our project was shovel-ready at the time that funding became available.

Even with that said, Customs changed their processes and asked that once we were almost done with the remodeling, that they were going to start checking all of the southbound trucks, and they would have random checks of southbound cars also. So with no more Federal funding available, Customs was very, very creative in coming up with and changing their budget to include 2 southbound lanes which were absolutely necessary. Those southbound lanes and that southbound inspection has—I don't know how many weapons and ammunition caches they have gotten, I don't know how much money they have gotten, but it has been in the millions of dollars' worth, and it has been extremely essential.

But with that said, we still don't have a port of entry. We have a brand-new port of entry, but it is understaffed by 300 agents. To be understaffed by 300 agents is absolutely not acceptable for the State of Arizona or for our country. The canine units, which to me would have been a little bit easier, we are at 20 canine units below what we should be.

So the funding may be getting to somewhere, but it is not getting to the border, and it is not getting to the line. We are losing more agents to attrition than we are in how fast we are hiring. We are not hiring fast enough.

Now, Congresswoman McSally has made changes in the billet so that the hiring process is a little bit more streamlined. That is a start. That is definitely a start. But the recognition, I think, is even more important that our ports are not adequate, whether they are in Long Beach in a sea port, or the Houston airport, or a Nogales port of entry. They are not efficient, not one bit whatsoever. If we were to have more efficient ports of entry, our economy would be booming. That is part of it.

Mr. PEARCE. I think that is probably my point when I said earlier that the systems are broken completely in Washington, because we are dedicating the resources, but they don't have enough internal discipline or process to see that the resources get where they need. So it gets very frustrating, and I appreciate your input.

Ms. Walden, you said that you all use the e-Verify now. As an employer in the oil field, my wife and I had a small business. We were frightened every day that we didn't have it and they would start charging us $10,000 a day.

Ms. STOCKHOLM WALDEN. Right, right.

Mr. PEARCE. Is the e-Verify actually working now?

Ms. STOCKHOLM WALDEN. You know, it has been very good. We were a little bit worried because we started very, very early, around the time of SB 1070, the State law, which we had problems with major provisions of, but we were a little worried that with the tremendous demand, as more and more employers used it, that it might break down. But, actually, it takes a couple of hours of training for your personnel or HR person, and we have a couple trained in it, and the one problem we have had occasionally, as you know, in the Hispanic culture there are often multiple names, and the maiden name as well as the surname of the father. So sometimes with multiple names and depending on how many they use, it might kick back somebody who is legal, but we usually just put it back through again and it works out, or it doesn't. But it really has helped tremendously, and we think that employers should be required to use that.

I think to Mr. Krentz' point earlier, the problem is when our grandparents came across, it didn't take 10 years to go through the process to be made legal. There is a problem. You weren't penalized for working during that time and forced into an underground economy while you were trying to get your paperwork for either temporary or permanent citizenship. So again, it goes to the efficiencies. You are absolutely right. But it definitely has an impact on business.

Mr. PEARCE. Again, I will re-look at that because I have been one of the ones who has been reluctant to have consequences for employers, because if your Government can't tell you who is legal and who is not illegal, how can you then push the responsibility down to employers? But if the e-Verify is starting to tighten up the process, then I will re-look at that.

Mr. Adams, I appreciate your heart for the human situation. I was left with a question as you testified. Would you contend for an open border? You compared it to North Carolina/South Carolina, and then the huddled masses wanting to come here. So I am just trying to clarify for myself that that would be your position, that you would favor just a plain open border?

Mr. ADAMS. I am here as a representative of the Presbyterian Church, as well as just as an individual.

Mr. PEARCE. Just you as an individual. I am not asking their position.

Mr. ADAMS. I can't separate that right now. The policy of the Presbyterian Church is in the written testimony. That would state that nations have the right to determine who enters and doesn't. My contention would agree with that and to make that a safe and efficient way that folks can come through ports of entry and not go through deserts.

Mr. PEARCE. I would ask Mr. Bell, but I think I know the answer. Is the barbed-wire fence more effective than the 12-foot-high fence?

Mr. BELL. Just to answer a previous question that you asked to the other panel, yes, we do have those smuggler signs, smuggler and illegal activity in the area. So we have that on our ranch, actually. As people go in and recreate, they get to see those.

But it will be interesting to find out because we got the 2-mile border wall that had a road constructed alongside of it. They just completed that extension road of 2 miles along the barbed-wire section, which there is no funding to do a border wall. So it will be interesting to see what happens. But the technology has been placed in the area.

I will tell you, even before the things were turned on, we were seeing differences in patterns of folks coming through. Granted, it was getting pushed over to the western portion of the ranch onto some of our neighbors, but it was coming, people could see it. They could see the road systems coming, and they are looking to stay away. That is not to say they are not coming through, but they are being detected.

So we have had a couple of drug seizures and vehicles due to the cameras picking things up. Some people who are crossing illegally are getting picked up along the way. So it has definitely made a difference.

Time is going to tell, but it is my contention that if you can get down there and patrol the border, regardless of whether it is the 18-foot fence, the south fence, or the barbed-wire fence, being able to patrol the border is going to make the difference. That is what is going to make the difference.

Mr. PEARCE. Okay.

Madam Chair, I just have a couple of quick questions, and they don't need very long answers.

Mr. Chamberlain, the X-ray units that are there, do you have them here in Nogales, and are they working? They are supposed to X-ray the entire truck and just see in a second if they need to pull it out of the line and then tear it apart. Are those working? Do you have them here?

Mr. CHAMBERLAIN. We do have them here. At the new port of entry we do. They do about 7 trucks in about 90 seconds, something like that. So they are much more efficient. We process during our peak season anywhere between 1,600 and 1,800 trucks a day. We have the capability at the brand-new port of entry to process over 4,000 trucks a day. Hopefully, as a businessman, that is my goal, to get to that, to get to max capacity for our port of entry. But if we don't have the staffing for it, there is no use. You can have all the technology you want and at the end of the day you still need the staffing for it. There is a human instinct about contraband, and you still need that. Machines can't do everything.

Mr. PEARCE. I would ask where the doubling of funding went and how come it didn't go to the Nogales port. Anyway, you got that out of the way at least.

Mr. CHAMBERLAIN. Thank you. I appreciate that.

[Laughter.]

Mr. PEARCE. Mr. Krentz, your father helped people who were coming across, gave them water, gave them food. Is that more or less correct?

Mr. KRENTZ. Yes.

Mr. PEARCE. They knew that, the people on the other side of the border. They know who is over here.

Mr. KRENTZ. Yes. We also, growing up, even when my dad was growing up, we had dealings with the ranchers on the other side. We would trade cattle across, bought cattle at the Mexican border there in Agua Prieta. We have been in the area a long time. But just like you said earlier, with the cartels coming in, the whole mentality of who is there and what their morals are has changed as well.

Mr. PEARCE. That is right. So did you all have a feeling that was retaliatory for turning in groups or whatever?

Mr. KRENTZ. Oh, I would hope not, but I don't know. I think it was more about——

Mr. PEARCE. You don't think people on the other side said, okay, if you are going to cooperate with law enforcement, we are coming to get you? You don't think——

Mr. KRENTZ. No. I think the guy that was probably involved was probably just not a good person.

Mr. PEARCE. Just a single instance of——

Mr. KRENTZ. Yes. But the reason that he was there was not because he was trying to find a hotel cleaning job.

Mr. PEARCE. Right. Okay.

Madam Chair, thank you very much. I would yield back. I appreciate the opportunity.

Ms. MCSALLY. Thank you, Mr. Pearce.

I want to highlight—you mentioned the waste, a lot of waste of money. There has been significant waste of resources put into a lot of good ideas. One of my 7 bills that passed the House is called the Border Technology Accountability Act. It is, as we speak, awaiting movement in the Senate. We could get this thing on the President's desk, which is basically intended to provide oversight and accountability to procurement programs for border technology. I mean, this is common-sense stuff to make sure we are good stewards of taxpayers' money, and it was unanimously passed in the House. We expected it to slide through. We thought it would be law by now, but somebody—there is evidently a Democrat holding it up in the Senate and not letting it go through. The intel that we were getting is a statement along the lines of they don't want to see Republicans get a win on anything related to border.

This is part of the dysfunction in Washington, DC. This is something everybody could agree upon, let's be good stewards of taxpayer resources. So I would encourage whoever is holding up that bill that they need to get it to the President's desk because this is an important thing for us to be able to do.

I just have one final—I want to be respectful of everybody's time, but I do want to give this panel an opportunity to comment on the interior checkpoints and the defense-in-depth strategy from your perspectives, and the implications of that and what your opinions are of that strategy.

I will start with Mr. Krentz.

Mr. KRENTZ. Thank you. I live on one of the only highways north of the border that doesn't have a checkpoint. I have been told or heard that that is so that they can go through, get out of the populated areas and get on their way, and then they will catch them somewhere on the interior side.

On the fixed checkpoints, I have also heard agents say that they know that they will unload before the checkpoints, walk around the checkpoints, and then get picked up afterwards. Like Del Cueto said earlier, the Darwinian people, they are the ones who are the only ones to get caught there at the checkpoint.

Ms. MCSALLY. Yes, that was my statement.

[Laughter.]

Mr. KRENTZ. So I have seen them as they—it is just kind-of like the wall. Is it the stopping point? No. But it is a deterrent to kind of slow them down and maybe catch them somewhere else. But that is about all.

Ms. MCSALLY. Ms. Walden.

Ms. STOCKHOLM WALDEN. We recommended in our citizens report roving checkpoints. We think that those are a lot more effective, by surprise. Change them up, switch them up. Again, Dick has shared with me the excellent infrared capabilities they had with airplanes when he flew the OV–1 Mohawk in Vietnam. I am sure it is light years ahead of that today. So we should be using things like that and not spending $200 million on Spy Net that could have been shot out, by the way, all those towers, by a BB gun, let alone a shotgun. It was the most ridiculous idea.

So, we are all for accountability, and congratulations to you on furthering that in the bill.

Finally, I just want to say, having come from the recent hearing on Federal lands, my understanding is that Border Patrol and other Federal agencies, other Federal law enforcement, as well as local law enforcement, have full access to Federal lands, whether they are in hot pursuit or not, if they have any suspicion of criminal activity. A lot of our friends who are ranchers in the group, like Warner and Wendy Glenn, the late Wendy Glenn, were concerned about more roads in wilderness areas, not just for the aesthetics but because they would be used by the traffickers.

So I think I am going to leave that to the people who have ranches along the border. I think there are areas where it is appropriate. But like Dan said, the train is so complex. I mean, this is not an easy fix. So just be aware of that, that you have to get a lot of local input as to whether you are making the problem better or worse.

Ms. McSALLY. Thank you.

Mr. CHAMBERLAIN. The depth strategy for us in the produce industry is a little bit cumbersome. The checkpoint there as you come south to north, you can see where the trucks have really, really done a tremendous job on the highway there. You have the ruts in the road that are absolutely terrible. Someone has to be able to pay for that. I don't know if that is going to be a Federal issue or that is going to be a State issue. But regardless, someone should have thought of that before they did the checkpoint at that point.

Also the land values, and I completely understand the businessmen that have suffered with the reduction of their business values and their land values, and their home values. That is difficult for us. You have to understand that for us, this is a tremendous freight corridor, an extremely important freight corridor for our country to move goods and services, whether it is the Madora business or the cattle business or the mining business or the produce industry. We are moving a tremendous amount of commerce through this highway here from Nogales to where we get to our major arteries in the Tucson and Phoenix areas.

So I think it is extremely important to patrol these areas just as much as we do in the rural parts of the State but in an effective way. I don't see the checkpoints being that effective. They are cumbersome. We have businesses from all over the United States and chain stores and food service companies coming to pick up our product from all over the United States, and they don't get this in other States around the country. They don't have to go through these checkpoints in other States. In California you do, in Texas you do, in Arizona and in New Mexico you do. I don't see that happening on the Northern Border. You have occasional checkpoints on the Northern Border, but they are nowhere as cumbersome to business and to tourism in the way that they are here.

Ms. McSALLY. Thank you.

Pastor Adams.

Mr. ADAMS. The policy from our church says border protection policies, we advocate the border protection policies that are consistent with humanitarian values and with the need to treat all individuals with respect while allowing the authorities to carry out the critical task of identifying and preventing entry of terrorists and dangerous criminals, as well as pursuing the legitimate task of implementing American immigration policy.

For me, the checkpoints have been a very effective tool for me to realize that not everyone is treated with the same respect as I am going through checkpoints. I think racial profiling—growing up in South Carolina, it was easy for me to not think about that, believe it or not. But now, with a family who have folks who both have the same complexion I do, as well as folks who are darker-complexioned, when we go through that checkpoint outside of Tombstone, we make sure I am driving and not my wife, Miriam. We were going through that checkpoint one time with my sister-in-law, who was in the back, and we just got waved right through. My sister-in-law said, hey, that is white privilege.

So checkpoints, there are lots of problems that you have heard about here, but one of the things about checkpoints is that it highlights that we have a long way to go in this country regarding race and treating everyone with respect.

Ms. McSALLY. Thanks, Pastor Adams.

Mr. Bell.

Mr. BELL. Well, I would like to kind-of start out with your defense-in-depth issue. The problem is in areas like my ranch and some of the stuff in the borderlands area, there is no access to the border. It is something I have been talking about quite a bit today. So that is the only option that is out there, unless you get horse patrols going in or helicoptering people in. Those are basically the only options you have. That is why it is important to be able to get that access and get down there.

The technology piece is important in that whereas before we had seismic sensors set out—we still do, but a sensor here would come on, and an agent would have no idea what that sensor hit was. Was it one of my cows? Was it a big mule deer? He has to maybe hump in 2 hours in his day to go figure out what that sensor hit was.

Technology is going to help in some of these areas to identify what that sensor hit was. Focus in on those areas where the sensor hits are happening. See what you can pick up. If it is a legitimate reason for an agent to go in, to maybe go in and apprehend a smuggler or a group, then they are going to know that is what it is instead of wasting time on something that isn't. So I think that is going to free up resources. But again, that all comes with deploying down closer to the area.

So the defense-in-depth strategy, I would like to see that go away, but in a lot of instances that is the only thing that is available because some of the roads are backed up 3, 4, 5, 6, 7 miles away from the border. So that is what our focus needs to be.

As far as the checkpoint, it is one of those deals where it is at that chokepoint. So they can get the traffic coming off the interstate, but they also have the mountain ranges on the flanks that is kind of choking things in. So they have a lot of technology on either side of that checkpoint, so they do make a lot of apprehensions in that area.

So for now, I think it is a necessity, but let's focus on getting down to the border, to the line of scrimmage, as you say. I agree with you. Then see where we are with that checkpoint at a later date.

Ms. McSally. Great. Thank you.

Mr. Pearce, do you have any more?

Mr. Pearce. Well, I just would like, again, to thank you very much.

I would like to thank the audience. People always wonder where a republic democracy begins. It begins right here, really. I have heard several people today say that we need to have the solutions coming from here towards Washington. I agree with that totally.

So again, Madam Chair, thanks for the invitation today, and thanks to our panelists. Both panels have just been outright stunning. So, thank you very much. I will carry these messages back to Washington.

Ms. McSally. Absolutely. I want to say thanks for joining us here and I appreciate you taking your time and your interest in these issues as our adjoining Congressional district.

I know there are other Members of the Committee that did want to be here. They do have your testimony. It is in the record. They may have some written questions for you, so we will keep the record open for 10 days and ask for you to respond in writing, if you don't mind, for that.

I do want to thank the audience for everybody's patience and endurance to be able to listen to these important issues. It took almost 3 hours here, but these are complex issues. They are not going to be solved in a 15-second sound bite, so I appreciate you all coming to listen.

I really appreciate both panels, all of you on the second panel, for providing your unique and important perspectives.

I just want to say it is an honor to be in this position. We have never had anybody chair this subcommittee before from Arizona, to be in this position that we can highlight what these issues are so we can find common ground and solutions to these issues that are impacting our public safety, our economy, and really all aspects of the lives that have been reflected in our community here.

I like to make decisions based on facts. It comes from basically serving in the military. Let's figure out what we know, what we don't know, and then figure out how to fix the problems that we are facing. I think we can all agree that our border is not as secure as it needs to be, that this is a public safety issue, that we need to make sure that as we are securing the border we are doing it at the ports of entry and between the ports of entry, and that we continue to have opportunities for commerce to grow because our economic opportunities as a border community are just as important as security, and we need to do both of those at the same time.

So we have a lot of follow-ups to do from this, but I really appreciate these perspectives so we can make fact-based determinations about how to move forward in the role that Congress has, which is a very important oversight role to the Federal agencies responsible for keeping our country and communities safe.

With that, let's make sure I have done all the admin here. I want to again thank the town of Sahuarita for allowing us to use this facility.

Pursuant to Committee Rule 7(e), the hearing record will be held open for 10 days.

Without objection, the subcommittee now stands adjourned.

[Whereupon, at 12:56 p.m., the subcommittee was adjourned.]

○